THE FOOD OF
THAILAND

Authentic Recipes from the Golden Kingdom

Recipes by *Sven Krauss, Laurent Ganguillet and Vira Sanguanwong*
Photography by *Luca Invernizzi Tettoni*
Introduction by *William Warren*
Editing by *Wendy Hutton*
Produced in association with *The Beaufort Sukhothai*

PERIPLUS
EDITIONS

Distributed in the Continental United States by The Crossing Press

Contents

Part One: Food in Thailand

*"In the water there are fish,
in the fields there is rice."*

Thus reads a celebrated stone inscription credited to King Ramkhamhaeng of Sukhothai, the first independent Thai kingdom founded in the early 13th century. It testifies to a natural abundance that was to sustain a series of capitals down the length of the fertile Chao Phraya River valley and also, more specifically, to the two mainstays of the Thai diet both then and now.

Rice culture came with the earliest settlers, long before the Thais themselves arrived on the scene, and led to a vast complex of paddy fields watered by an intricate system of canals, rivers and reservoirs. Fish were equally plentiful, not only in the myriad waterways but also in the seas.

To these basic ingredients, readily available to all, were gradually added others, drawn over the centuries from a wide variety of cultures: some nearby, like China and India, some remote like Persia and Portugal. Even such seemingly essential elements as the pungent chili pepper were, in fact, introductions from distant South America. However they came, though, they were subtly modified and refined into a cuisine distinctively Thai, not quite like any other in the world.

The diverse glories of classic Thai cooking long remained unappreciated by the outside world. Alone among the countries of Southeast Asia, Thailand remained independent during the era of colonization; thus, relatively few Westerners sampled its unique blends of hot and sweet, sour and salty—so different from the dishes of India, Malaya and Indonesia, despite their superficial similarity.

Even those who came for lengthy stays were rarely treated to the genuine fare. Restaurants catering to foreigners in larger cities like Bangkok tended until quite recently to be Chinese or European. For the most part, only in private homes could one sample delicate, traditional dishes that resulted from hours of preparation by skilled hands, using methods that had been handed down for generations.

All that, of course, has now changed dramatically. In the past decade or so, Thai food has become an international phenomenon, with countless restaurants now offering it from Sydney to Stockholm. Serious Western chefs find fresh inspiration in its flavors and techniques, and ordinary diners are discovering its remarkable diversity. In Thailand itself, regional variations are far more available than before, and there are now elegantly decorated establishments specializing in the refined art of "palace cooking."

Thai food, then, might be said to have entered a new era, one that will certainly bring an even wider appreciation of its many delights.

*Pages 4–5:
Monks file
through the
courtyard of a
temple in the
northern town
of Chiang Mai.*
Opposite:
*This charming
painting evokes
the life of the
village, where—
despite the
burgeoning of
Bangkok and
other cities—the
majority of Thais
still live.*

The Land and its People

*From rice fields to rubies: a country
as varied and complex as its people*

Images of Thailand among outsiders vary according to taste and temperament. To some, the country conjures up a *King and I* fantasy of gilded temples and palaces, to others a palm-fringed beach of snowy white sand, an exotic tribal village high in misty mountains or the brassy, big-city lure of Bangkok. All are valid enough as individual impressions, yet misleading in terms of the whole, for Thailand, like its food, is a complex mixture of flavors and the product of a unique history.

Covering some 198,500 square miles—roughly the size of France—it encompasses a wide range of topography. Mountains in the far north, where Thailand's borders meet those of Burma and Laos, rise to more than 8,000 feet, with verdant valleys and the remains of once-extensive teak forests.

The northeast consists of a rolling semi-arid plateau stretching all the way to the Mekong River, while the flat central plains, watered by the Chao Phraya River, form one of the richest rice-growing regions on earth. The narrow southern

Thailand's central plains form one of the richest rice-growing regions in the world.

isthmus, extending down to Malaysia, is bordered on one side by the Gulf of Thailand and on the other by the Indian Ocean, with a spine of rugged limestone mountains down the middle.

A largely benign climate allows year-round cultivation of crops, not only rice but also fruits and vegetables. Even today, despite the growth of urban areas, the great majority of the population can be found in villages of around 150 households (about 700 people) who derive their living from agriculture. Other natural resources include a variety of minerals, precious stones, such as rubies and sapphires, and an abundance of seafood along two long coastlines bordering the Indian Ocean to the west and the South China Sea to the east.

The Thais were not the first people drawn to this land of plenty. Evidence of settlers dating back to the Paleolithic Age, some 500,000 years ago, have been found in several parts of the country, and archaeologists exploring a cave near the Burmese border discovered the carbonized remains of such plants as Chinese water chestnut, bottle gourd and cucumber that were dated from 9,700 to 6,000 B.C. The most dramatic and extensive prehistoric remains have emerged in the northeast, where a remarkable culture flourished from around 4,000 B.C. to just after the start of the Christian Era, numbering among its achievements rice cultivation and sophisticated bronze metallurgy.

Indian traders later established ports along the southern peninsula, bringing not only Buddhism but numerous other cultural and culinary influences. Mon settlers arrived around the same time in the Chao Phraya valley and founded the Dvaravati kingdom, a major producer of rice as well as an important religious center. Their power was eventually replaced by that of the Khmers, whose empire once extended over the northeast and much of the central region.

The ethnic Thais, originating as a minority group in what is now southern China, gradually migrated southward in search of greater independence and better land for agriculture. The earliest groups settled in the far north, forming a loose federation of city states centered around Chiang Mai. Others ventured farther down, to the northern extremities of the central plains. By the 13th century, the Thais had established themselves in such numbers that they were eventually able to overthrow their Khmer overlords and establish a kingdom of their own.

This kingdom was called Sukhothai, which in Sanskrit means "Dawn of Happiness," and though its power lasted less than two centuries, its influence proved far more enduring. Under King Ramkham-

Food is all important in Thailand, whether it's for a religious festival or a farmer's midday meal in the shade at the edge of a paddy field.

haeng, the greatest Sukhothai ruler, the Thai alphabet was devised, splendid works of Buddhist art were created and a truly indigenous Thai culture emerged.

Ayutthaya, the next capital, began in 1350 as a small city-state on the Chao Phraya River and over the next 400 years became one of the most cosmopolitan cities in Southeast Asia. Countless new ingredients were added to the Thai cultural blend in this period, during which the first contacts were made with Europe and an active trade established with other Asian countries. At its peak in the late 17th century, Ayutthaya had a population greater than London, representing more than a dozen different cultures.

Less than a century later, Ayutthaya fell to an invading Burmese army, which proceeded to burn the great city and disperse most of its people. The Thais rallied with remarkable speed, however, and within the next fifteen years had managed to expel the Burmese and to establish a temporary capital farther down the river at Thonburi. In 1782, a dynamic young military leader assumed the throne as King Rama I, founded the present Chakri Dynasty, and moved the capital across the Chao Phraya to what is now Bangkok.

Right:
During the busy harvest season, when rice stalks are cut by hand and often threshed on the spot, the midday meal is carried to the fields for eating in some shady spot nearby.
Opposite:
Rice fields seen from the air are a checkerboard of black, green and gold.

kingdom's independence, Chinese immigrants who came in large numbers to the new city, as well as Western traders, added to its diversity. By the end of the 19th century, roads stretched far from the river banks and Bangkok was well on its way to becoming a modern, Western-style city—at least in appearance.

Change was more gradual in the countryside, where the age-old patterns continued to prevail. Indeed, some areas, such as the far north and the northeast, remained relatively isolated until well into the present century, preserving regional ways that included cooking as well as other aspects of culture. Even Bangkok, behind its facade, is still more Thai than many visitors might perceive, since it is for the most part composed of villagers attracted by city jobs but attuned to traditional ways.

Bangkok began as a conscious evocation of the lost capital of Ayutthaya. Many of the early palaces and temples were replicas of similar ones in the old capital; similarly, too, an intricate network of canals served as streets, crowded with boats of all kinds.

But with growing prosperity, this traditional Thai aspect soon changed dramatically. Though skilled Chakri rulers were able to maintain the

Famed for their dazzling smiles, love of fun and apparent adaptability, the Thais also have other traits, perhaps less evident to the casual observer: a toughness which enabled them to prevail over others who sought the same territory, a passion for independence and, most of all, a genius for absorbing outside influences while maintaining their own distinctive identity.

The Evolution of Thai Cuisine

The development of a unique and skillfully composed mosaic

Right:
A late 19th-century mural shows the traditional way of eating with the hand while seated on the floor.
Opposite:
The 13th-century kingdom of Sukhothai (Dawn of Happiness) produced magnificent works of Buddhist art.

One of the most notable characteristics of Thai decorative art is its passion for intricate detail, particularly apparent in complex mosaics of colored glass and porcelain that adorn so many religious buildings. From afar, these suggest a solid, seamless pattern; only on closer inspection are the separate components revealed, and the skillful way they have been put together.

It is easy to see an analogy between such mosaics and many aspects of Thai culture, including its cuisine. Here, too, a wide variety of elements have been brought together and artfully composed into something quite unique, often surprising in the effect that it creates.

Little is known about the cooking of Sukhothai, where so much of what we regard as distinctively Thai first emerged. From the information in King Ramkhamhaeng's famous inscription, however, it is clear that rice and fish were the major ingredients. Fruits were undoubtedly plentiful as well, along with mushrooms that grew wild in the forests and a variety of vegetables. One item not present,

however, was the now ubiquitous chili, which originated in Central and South America and did not appear in Asian cuisines until the arrival of the first Europeans, several centuries later.

A clearer picture is available of Ayutthaya, thanks largely to 17th-century French visitors who characteristically devoted a considerable amount of space to the subject of food in their accounts of the kingdom. Simon de la Loubere, for instance, who came with a diplomatic mission in 1687, was struck by the fact that the people ate sparingly. Good salt, he found, was a rare commodity, and fresh fish was seldom eaten, despite its abundance.

"A Siamese," he wrote, "makes a very good meal with a pound of rice a day, which amounts to not more than a farthing, and with a little dry or salt fish, which costs not much more...Their sauces are plain, a little water with some spices, garlic, or some sweet herb. They do very much esteem a liquid sauce, like mustard, which is only crayfish corrupted because they are ill-salted; they call it Kepi."

Nicolas Gervaise, a Jesuit missionary, noted that *kapi*, the popular fermented shrimp paste, "has such a pungent smell that it nauseates anyone not accustomed to it" and gives perhaps the first general recipe for a typical Thai condiment based on it: "salt, pepper, ginger, cinnamon, cloves, garlic, white onions, nutmeg and several strongly flavoured herbs...mixed in considerable quantities with this shrimp paste."

From these accounts it is clear that for all its seeming simplicity, Thai cooking was already becoming more sophisticated. The presence of cloves and nutmeg is evidence of trade with the East Indies, and the fact that numerous Chinese, Japanese, Malays and Indians lived in Ayutthaya suggests other likely influences. None of the French writers specifically mentions chilies, but they were probably already in use, either brought directly by the Portuguese, who opened relations in 1511, or having come via Malacca or India. The Portuguese were also responsible for a number of still popular Thai sweets based on sugar and egg yolks and possibly for introducing the tomato, which is of New World origin.

The complex seasonings we now regard as typical of Thai cuisine, including chilies, were certainly well established by the Rattanakosin, or Bangkok, period. This is made abundantly clear in an account by Sir John Bowring, who wrote in 1855: "The Siamese prepare considerable quantities of curry as their habitual food. These are generally so hot that they burn the mouth of a European."

Bowring obviously learned to appreciate some of the "ardent comestibles," among them the essential sauce called *nam prik*, which, he explained, "is prepared by bruising a small quantity of red pepper in a mortar, to which are added *kapi* (paste of shrimps or prawns), black pepper, garlic and onions. These being thoroughly mixed, a small quantity of brine and citron-juice is added. Ginger, tamarinds and gourd seeds are also employed. The *nam prik* is one of the most appetite-exciting condiments."

Rice noodles were probably common in Ayutthaya, part of the China's considerable culinary legacy, but they became even more so in Bangkok, enhanced with Thai flavors and popular as a luncheon dish. Vendors offered a quick meal of *kwaytiaow* (stir-fried noodles with vegetables and meat or shrimp) from boats along the canals that threaded the capital and still do on almost every sidewalk in the city.

Another, more refined type of cuisine prevailed in royal and aristocratic households. Sometimes referred to as "palace cooking," this entailed not only great skill at blending various ingredients to achieve the most subtle nuances of taste but also the ability to carve fruits and vegetables in a wide variety of decorative forms to enhance the appearance of a dish. The acknowledged center of such skills was the women's quarter of the Grand Palace, where many daughters of aristocratic families were sent to prepare them for future life.

Thai food today may still be plain or fancy, a dish that can be prepared in a few minutes over a charcoal brazier or one requiring hours of chopping, grinding and carving; it may vary considerably from region to region. Always, though, it remains a singular creation, not quite like any of the influences that have shaped it over the centuries.

Opposite:
Herbal medicines are still prepared according to prescriptions preserved in ancient manuscripts.

Regional Cooking

In a land of geographic diversity, distinctive variations on a basic theme

Perhaps the majority of foreign lovers of Thai food have acquired their taste for it in restaurants abroad, or during a visit limited largely to Bangkok. What many may fail to realize is that the country's cooking varies from region to region, sometimes in small ways that only a true expert could fully appreciate, sometimes in dramatic ways. A provincial journey can thus be a rewarding culinary experience as well as an opportunity to enjoy a variety of scenic attractions.

In the mountainous north, for instance, where borders are shared with Burma and Laos, the cuisine is as distinctive as the handicrafts for which the region is noted. Here, the earliest Thais settled on their migration southward from China, forming first a group of small city states and then a loose federation known as Lanna, with Chiang Mai as the principal city.

Over the years there were conflicts with both Burma and the rising Thai state of Ayutthaya in the Central Plains. Even after the Lanna kingdom came under the administrative control of Bangkok, it remained remote from the rest of the country until a railway was cut in 1921.

As a result of this long isolation, the north was able to retain much of its native culture: its language (as different from central Thai as Spanish is from Portuguese), its crafts (among them lacquer, silverware and fine woodcarving), its customs (such as placing a jar of cool water outside houses for thirsty passersby) and its food.

Instead of the soft, boiled rice of the central region, northerners prefer a steamed glutinous variety, rolled into small balls and dipped into liquid dishes. Curries of the region tend to be thinner, without the coconut milk so widely used in central and southern cooking. There is also a distinctive local version of Nam Prik Ong, a basic dipping sauce served with raw vegetables and crispy pork skin, as well as a pork sausage called Naem, eaten plain with rice or mixed into various dishes. When it is in season, the favorite local fruit is the succulent *longan*, which grows in almost every compound.

Opposite:
Kantoke, a meal taken while seated at a low round table, is a traditional way of dining in the north of Thailand.
Left:
Girls from the northern town of Lampang.

The influence of neighboring Burma and Laos is apparent in many northern dishes. The former, for example, was responsible for the popular Khao Soi, a curry broth with egg noodles and chicken, pork or beef, as well as Gaeng Hang Lay, a pork curry seasoned with ginger, tamarind and turmeric. Of Laotian origin are Nam Prik Noom, a sauce with a strong chili-lime flavor and Ook Gai, a red chicken curry with lemongrass.

The traditional form of entertainment in the north is the *kantoke* dinner, the name derived from *kan,* or "bowl," and *toke,* a low round table made of woven bamboo, plain or lacquered. Sitting on the floor around the table, guests help themselves to the assorted dishes placed on it and regularly replenished by the attentive hostess.

Like the north, northeastern Thailand was also long regarded as remote from the cosmopolitan world of Bangkok. In this case, however, the reason was not so much geography as a perceptible social prejudice on the part of city dwellers. Isan, as Thais call the northeast, was the poorest of the country's four main regions, with infertile soil and devastating droughts that frequently drove farmers to the capital in search of work as laborers, taxi drivers, domestic servants.

Finicky outsiders tended to look on Isan food as "strange," and some of the region's delicacies are certainly unusual when compared with the abundance of other areas: grubworms and grasshoppers, for instance, ant eggs, snail curry and fermented fish of exceptional pungency. But increasingly, other less exotic dishes typical of the region have won widespread admiration, to the point where they now appear on the menus of smart Bangkok restaurants and are savored by the most discriminating Thai food connoisseurs. Some diners, indeed, look upon a properly prepared Som Tam (spicy green papaya salad) or Laab (even spicier minced pork or chicken) as being the true marks of a superior Thai cook, wherever he may be plying his trade.

If the people of Isan "eat anything," as residents of other regions often remark, they have a definite skill for transforming it in ways that show both imagination and ingenuity. Barbecued chicken or Gai Yang, is grilled with a healthy lashing of peppery sauce and garlic, while catfish is the base of a delectable curry and Laab Dip is made with raw meat and roasted rice powder.

For Haw Mok, fish is ground with curry paste and then steamed in banana leaf to make a many-flavored custard. Beef—a relatively rare commodity—is marinated and grilled, and any leftovers are com-

Fresh mushrooms found growing wild in the forests are now joined by several varieties of cultivated mushroom.

bined with fresh mint, green onions, and chilies for a fiery salad. Perhaps because chilies add such a zip to the most mundane dish, northeasterners tend to use them with a greater abandon than Thais of other areas.

Much northeastern cooking reflects the influence of Laos just across the Mekong River—not surprizingly since many residents are ethnically Lao. Dill (called *pak chee Lao* or "Laotian coriander" by Thais) is widely used as a garnish, and glutinous rice is preferred to the normal variety. Also of Lao origin and popular on festive occasions is Khanom Buang, a crispy crepe stuffed with dried shrimp, bean sprouts, and other ingredients.

Southern Thailand consists of a slender peninsula stretching down to Malaysia, dramatically different from the rest of the country in both scenery and culture. Lush jungle clambers up craggy limestone mountains, nurtured by rain that falls for eight months of the year, and cultivated areas tend to be vast rubber and coconut plantations rather than the familiar rice fields and fruit orchards of the central plains. From villages along two long coastlines—one on the Gulf of Thailand, the other on the Indian Ocean—thousands of boats sail out to fish the surrounding waters, bringing back seafood for local consumption and profitable export.

Highly distinctive visually is the domed mosque, for the south is home to most of Thailand's two million Muslims, its largest religious minority. These are concentrated in the provinces adjacent to Malaysia, where Malay is spoken as commonly as Thai. In other southern places like Songkhla and the island of Phuket, Chinese predominate and lend their own particular color to the local scene.

Southern food reflects most of these features, cultural and otherwise, as well as others from its more distant past when traders from India and Java sailed to its numerous ports. The graceful coconuts to be seen growing so plentifully everywhere provide milk for thickening soups and curries, oil for frying and grated flesh as a condiment for many dishes.

From the seas come huge marine fish, rock lobsters, crabs, mussels, squid, prawns and scallops, while local plantations yield cashew nuts, which turn up regularly as an appetizer or garnish, and small but juicy pineapples, which provide a popular sweet at the end of a meal.

Seafood may be prepared simply, grilled or steamed; or more elaborately, baked in a claypot with thin noodles and garlic; or as the main component of Tom Yam, that ubiquitous Thai soup laced

Northeastern or Isan food, once looked on with suspicion by other Thais, has now gained wide acceptance.

The Isthmus of Kra in southern Thailand is bathed by the Andaman Sea and the waters of the Gulf of Thailand, providing a magnificent variety of seafood.

bamboo skewers with a spicy peanut sauce.

The fourth of the country's regions, the Central Plains, is the Thai heartland: a vast checkerboard of paddy fields, orchards and vegetable gardens, with Bangkok as the principal market and cultural magnet. The best rice comes from here, pearly white and fragrant, and so do the best fruits—mangoes and durians, ruby-red mangosteens and hairy rambutans, crisp guavas, papayas and pomelos, even grapes in a special tropical hybrid. Vegetables, eaten in large quantities, include cabbage, mushrooms, morning glory (water spinach), cucumber, tomatoes and pumpkins, as well as more recent introductions like asparagus and baby corn.

Food in the villages that stand like islands amid the fields tends to be plain: rice with stir-fried vegetables, fish from a nearby canal or river, perhaps some minced chicken with garlic, chilies and basil and a salad of salted eggs, chilies and spring onion with a squeeze of lime.

In Bangkok, of course, everything is available, even the most exotic regional delicacies, if one knows where to look. The capital is also the place for the creations known as "palace cooking," distinguished for their elegant presentation and served only in the best restaurants. Perhaps most typical of the city's culinary offerings, however, are the many fast foods based on Chinese noodles, prepared at a moment's notice at any sidewalk cafe or by vendors who push their carts along residential streets. Tasty, nourishing, occasionally even distinguished, these quick meals epitomize the busy life of Bangkok and also the Thai capacity for making something special out of the simplest ingredients.

with lemongrass and chilies. In general, southerners like their food chili-hot, and are fond of a bitter taste imparted by a flat, native bean called *sataw*, which other Thais tend to find less appealing.

Contributions from other cultures include Gaeng Mussaman, an Indian-style curry with cardamom, cloves, cinnamon and either chicken or beef; Malay fish curries, often with a garnish of fresh fruit; and Indonesian satay, marinated bits of meat on

A Moveable Feast

Food vendors and their role in everyday life

First come the pile drivers to lay the foundations for one of the huge new buildings that seem to be rising on almost every street in Bangkok and other major cities. The workers follow, setting up a collection of temporary shacks on or near the site. And then, often simultaneously, the food vendors appear, ready to supply a quick, cheap, above all convenient meal to anyone who happens to crave one. A Thai city street without vendors is as hard to imagine as one devoid of traffic.

As a result of this widespread interest, Thai street food has evolved into a distinctive culinary category all its own, generally characterized by speed of preparation (if any is done on the spot) and easy portability of equipment and roughly divided into snacks and more substantial fare.

Snacks cover a wide range. Some may consist of nothing more than freshly sliced fruit sprinkled with salt, sugar, dried chilies or a combination of these seasonings. Or they may be a selection of traditional sweets, prepared by the vendor at home and temptingly arranged in a display case. Other vendors offer noodle creations adequate for a fast, nourishing lunch. To produce the universally popular *kwaytiaow*, a bowl of freshly cooked rice noodles is given a few ladles of meat stock, topped with precooked pork or chicken, and sprinkled with sugar, crushed peanuts and dried chili flakes, while for Pad Thai the noodles are quickly stir-fried with garlic, spring onions, salty dried shrimp and a variety of spices.

Gai Yang, northeastern-style barbecued chicken, is grilled over a charcoal brazier and often served with side orders of glutinous rice and green papaya salad.

Just about every governor of Bangkok has tried, at some point in his tenure, to outlaw food vendors, citing civic hygiene, sidewalk obstruction and general untidiness. All have failed for the simple reason that the vendors fill a clearly perceived need for a substantial number of city residents. Were the opportunity for a quick meal to be taken away, as one fan wrote indignantly to a local newspaper, "it would be the end of civilisation as we know it."

An artist's impressions of "food to go" in Thailand, where pushcarts and street stalls are an essential part of everyday life.

Palace Cuisine

Within the palace walls: refinements of the royal cuisine

It "was a town complete in itself, a congested network of houses and narrow streets, with gardens, lawns, artificial lakes and shops. It had its own government, its own institutions, its own laws and law-courts. It was a town of women, controlled by women."

Dr. Malcolm Smith, who served as physician to some members of the Thai royal family in the early years of this century, was describing the innermost part of Bangkok's mile-square Grand Palace known as the "Inside," where the women of the court lived. At its peak, during the reign of King Rama V, the "Inside" had a population estimated at nearly 3,000, a select few of them bearing the exalted rank of Queen but the great majority ladies-in-waiting and lower attendants.

The "Inside" was misunderstood by many outsiders, particularly foreign missionaries, who viewed it as the most obvious manifestation of polygamy, an institution of which they strongly disapproved. Even a few outsiders who were granted entry, like Anna Leonowens, insisted on referring to it as "the harem," its female guards as "Amazons," and its inhabitants as quasi-prisoners. This view actually had a lot more to do with Western fantasies than with fact.

In truth, the inner palace can be more accurately viewed as a kind of ultra-exclusive finishing school, a place where the most refined aristocratic skills were perfected and passed on. The daughter of a nobleman who had spent all or part of her youth in this rarefied atmosphere was regarded as highly desirable by any future husband, for she would surely be adept at supervising an elegant household of her own in the outside world.

During their ample leisure time, the royal women learned such delicate arts as traditional Thai floral decoration, threading fragrant blossoms into intricate wreaths and molding clay into miniature dolls of marvelous detail. Above all, they learned how to prepare various foods that were not merely more subtle in flavor than their outside versions but

Hours of painstaking effort and great skill are needed to produce the exquisite fruit and vegetable carvings which are a hallmark of palace cuisine.

highly memorable in visual appeal.

The hallmarks of the so-called "palace food"—which was, in fact, to be found in most aristocratic homes as well—were painstaking hours of preparation and an artistic sense of presentation. Foi Thong, for instance, is a blend of egg yolks and sugar transformed into a nest of silky golden threads, while Look Choop are tiny imitation fruits shaped by hand from a mixture of bean paste and coconut milk and colored to exactly match their real-life models. Mee Grob, which one writer has called "the epitome of palace cuisine," involves crisp rice noodles and shrimp in a sweet-sour sauce, so time-consuming to make properly that it was once seldom found in restaurants.

The most visible of palace skills was the art of fruit and vegetable carving. Watermelons, mangoes, tomatoes, pumpkins, spring onions, chilies, ginger root and innumerable other garnishes and delicacies became realistic flowers, leaves and abstract designs through the deft use of a knife, sometimes requiring as long to prepare as the dishes that they adorned.

Royal polygamy ended under King Rama VI. A few resisted relocation—at least one was still in residence as late as the 1960s—but gradually, the ladies of the "Inside" and their numerous attendants left their protected existence and entered another, very different one outside the high walls. Even today, the once-teeming streets and elegant palaces are closed to most outsiders, though some women continue to come and, sitting in the shade of venerable trees, continue to make the beautiful garlands and other flower arrangements presented by the

Five-colored porcelain or Bencharong wares seen in the fore-ground of a corner of Vimarn Mek Palace were specially created in China to meet Thai tastes.

royal family at the countless ceremonies over which they preside.

Fortunately, though, palace cooking did not vanish along with the hidden world where it originated. It survived through the descendants of the royal women and, especially in recent years, has been discovered by a wider public through several restaurants that take pride in their re-creations of this unique cuisine.

Eating Thai

The etiquette and enjoyment of a Thai meal

Wherever it is eaten—in a restaurant, on a city sidewalk, on the open verandah of a farm house, even in the middle of a rice field at harvest time—a Thai meal is nearly always a social affair. Today, in most urban areas, a table and chairs are likely to be used for dining, though the floor still suffices in many rural homes, covered with several soft reed mats. Moreover, Western cutlery has come into general use: not knives, for in a properly prepared Thai meal nothing is large enough to need cutting, but a large spoon to scoop up individual portions of rice and a fork to help move the food on one's plate.

In the north and northeast, where steamed glutinous rice is preferred, it is proper to use the fingers to form small balls and dip them into more liquid dishes. Chopsticks may also be provided for Chinese-style noodle dishes, and a ceramic Chinese spoon for soups and certain desserts.

A large container of rice is always the centerpiece. Around this are placed all the other dishes and condiments, with the possible exception of dessert, if one is served. Guests are free to help themselves, in any order they want, mixing dishes at will and seasoning them with a wide variety of condiments to achieve the desired taste. The soup may thus be eaten at either the beginning or the end of a meal, and the salad likewise. The only constants are the rice, which accompanies almost everything, and dessert, which is usually brought after the other dishes have been removed.

The ideal Thai meal aims at being a harmonious blend of the spicy, the sweet and the sour, and is meant to be satisfying to the eye, nose and palate. Sometimes several of these flavors are subtly blended in a single dish, while sometimes one predominates. In addition to the rice, a typical meal might include a soup, a curry or two, a salad, a fried dish and a steamed one.

There will also be a considerable variety of sauces and condiments: *nam pla*, the essential salt substitute made from fermented fish; *nam prik*, which is *nam pla* combined with chopped chilies and other ingredients; crushed dried chilies as well as fresh ones for those who like their food really hot; pickled garlic; locally made chili sauce, and such fresh vegetables as cucumbers, tomatoes and spring onions.

The most common dessert is one or more of the delectable fruits that are so abundant in Thailand, while on special occasions, more elaborate desserts such as Foi Thong ("golden threads") or banana-leaf cups of Takaw, a confection of tapioca starch, sugar and coconut that comes in a wide variety of forms, may be served.

***Opposite**:
A table for two is more likely to be found in a restaurant than in a family home, where dining is a sociable experience shared by many.*

Part Two: The Thai Kitchen

Despite the advent of modern methods and utensils,
some traditional implements are still regarded as irreplaceable

Of the various basic implements used in the preparation of Thai food, a number have remained essentially unchanged over the years. Others have been replaced by cheaper (but not always more efficient) modern devices and are now mainly to be seen in antique shops, objects admired for their beauty of form but no longer serving a practical purpose for the modern Thai cook.

In a traditional Thai home of the not-very-distant past, the kitchen was nearly always a separate structure from the main house, its central feature being an often smoky stove. Lacking gas or electricity, the fuel was usually charcoal, or wood when it was readily available as in forested areas like the north. There are still many noted Thai cooks who insist that only charcoal can provide the desired quality of heat for certain dishes and who maintain a small brazier along with the gas and electric cookers that have become standard equipment, at least in city households.

The oldest kind of stove, now virtually extinct, was an ingenious device called a *cherng kran*, a rimmed earthenware tray with one side raised to hold the bottom of a cooking pot; the fuel was placed under the pot on the tray. This had the advantages of requiring little space and of being easily moved from place to place (just as the traditional Thai house, made of prefabricated sections, could also be taken down and transferred to a new site with comparatively little effort). The *cherng kran* later gave way to more substantial, but still portable, charcoal cookers and finally to built-in ranges made of tiled cement, perhaps reflecting the tendency of the Thais themselves to stay put as permanent towns and cities developed.

The actual cooking of most Thai dishes, past and present, is done with remarkable speed and employs only a small number of utensils, the most important of them being a few wok-like iron pans of varying sizes, a spatula with a rounded edge to stir the food around, and assorted pots for boiling.

Far more time, however, must be spent on the preliminary preparation of various ingredients, which have to be peeled, chopped, grated, ground,

Opposite:
Floating markets, where everything the housewife might need is piled into small boats and paddled along canals and rivers, are a common sight in the Chao Phraya delta.
Left:
Although aesthetically more appealing, terracotta utensils such as these are today largely replaced by metal pans.

blended and marinated, essential procedures that can take many hours for some creations and that led to the evolution of many special tools.

One of the most decorative of these was the *kude maprow* or **coconut grater**. This probably began as a simple seat, at one end of which was a sharp iron grater and below, a tray to receive the shredded coconut meat, all often carved from a single piece of wood. The user straddled the seat and, leaning forward, rotated half a coconut around the teeth of the grater in a process that looked easier than it was—the smallest slip could result in a painful cut. The *kude maprow* eventually became much more elaborate, with the seat carved in various shapes, usually that of a rabbit (perhaps because of the protruding teeth) but also other animals or humans, and displaying considerable artistry. Today these are comparatively rare and much prized by collectors, though some sort of scraping device is still needed, along with another to render the coconut "milk" that forms the base of so many Thai recipes.

Thai housewives with access to a market can buy freshly grated coconut, taking it home to squeeze with water to make fresh coconut milk. Cooks living outside of Asia and far from the nearest electric coconut grinder must content themselves with substitutes such as packaged flaked coconut or canned coconut cream.

Other classic implements have proved more durable than the coconut grater. The *krok* and *saak*, or **mortar and pestle**, traditionally made of stone or wood but also available in baked clay or metal, is still vital for all the grinding and pounding of spices that produce the distinctive flavors of Thai food. Usually there are two of these, one deep for up and down pounding and another, flatter, for grinding.

Although many traditionally minded cooks swear that modern food processors or blenders cannot provide the same results as a mortar and pestle, most Western cooks would be prepared to trade speed and ease of preparation for the laborious old method. If using a blender to grind such items as shallots, garlic, chilies, lemongrass and so on, be sure to chop or slice all items first, and to blend the tougher ingredients (galangal, lemongrass) before adding the softer ones. Add a little of the cooking medium (oil, coconut milk or water) specified in the recipe, to help keep the blades turning if necessary.

There are, however, no really satisfactory substitutes for the thick wooden **chopping block** and sharp **cleaver** used in both heavy-duty and delicate cutting. These are readily available in most Asian specialty stores.

Another important adjunct to the Thai kitchen is a **wire-mesh basket** with a long handle of wood or bamboo, used to lower foods into oil for deep-

Above:
*Traditional coconut scrapers are increasingly rare, although wire-mesh baskets (**below right**), are still indispensable.*

frying, to plunge noodles into boiling water and to blanch vegetables. These come in a number of forms, depending on the use—shallow for frying, deeper for holding noodles and vegetables, and are available at every market. (Similar items can be found in Western stores, not as attractive, perhaps, but serving the same purpose.)

Equally essential for preparing many basic dishes is some sort of **steamer**. Often today this is made of metal and may even be electric, though in provincial areas it is still more likely to be traditional—a set of bamboo trays, for instance, which are stacked over boiling water with a cover on the top one; or, in the north and northeast, an elegant footed utensil known as a *kong khao*, which can be used both for steaming glutinous rice and also for carrying it while traveling or working in the fields.

In addition to these, there are more exotic devices difficult to find outside Thailand, each used for a very specific purpose. One, the *ka po*, consists of three-quarters of a coconut shell, in the bottom of which are drilled small holes; two parallel rods are attached with rattan to either side of the top so that the shell can be placed on a pot of boiling water. Rice-flour, tapioca, or mung bean paste is poured into the bowl and pressed to produce a noodle-like

sweet, which is then sieved and served cold. A simpler variation is the *la-chong*, a perforated metal plate that looks like a cheese grater, through which the paste is pressed.

Several brass or bronze implements are also commonly used to make some of the more complex sweets. A cone with two small openings facilitates the production of the classic Foi Thong, or "golden threads," a delicate egg-yolk creation thought to have been introduced by the Portuguese during the Ayutthaya period. A sauce dispenser with a small hole (such as the Kikkoman soy sauce bottle) makes an acceptable substitute, although it takes a fair amount of practice to create these "golden threads."

Another unusual utensil is a shell-shaped mold, usually made of brass, with a long wooden handle. The mold is dipped first into hot oil and then into batter; it is plunged back into the oil and the batter cooks to form delicate crisp little cups. These cups or *krathong* are filled to make delightful savory snacks. (Similar snacks known as *kuih pi tee* are found in neighboring Malaysia and Singapore.)

Some of these implements have now made their way into Western cookery shops specializing in Asian cuisine. While reasonable substitutes can be found for most of the others, the pleasure of a visit to Thailand can be enhanced by plunging into a colorful market and finding the genuine article, which can later be put to practical use.

Above: *A bamboo strainer and woven storage baskets (**below left**) are as attractive as they are practical.*

Thai Ingredients

Essential ingredients for the true taste of Thailand

AGAR-AGAR: A gelatin derived from seaweed which gels desserts and cakes without refrigeration. To use, sprinkle powdered agar-agar over liquid and bring it gently to a boil, stirring until dissolved. One teaspoon sets approximately $1-1\frac{1}{2}$ cups of liquid.

BAMBOO SHOOTS *(naw mai)*: The fresh shoots of several varieties of bamboo make an excellent vegetable. They must first be peeled, sliced and simmered for about 30 minutes until tender. If using canned bamboo shoots, remove any metallic taste by draining the shoots, then boiling them in fresh water for 5 minutes.

BASIL: The most commonly used basil, fairly similar to European and American sweet basil, is known as *horapa*; it is used liberally as a seasoning and sprigs of it are often added to platters of fresh raw vegetables. Similar yet paler in color and with a distinctive lemony fragrance, "lemon basil" or *manglak* is used in soups and salads. *Kaprow*, sometimes known as "holy basil," is rarely used.

BEAN CURD: Several types of bean curd or tofu are used in Thailand. Soft white bean curd *(tau hoo)* is often steamed or added to soups, while small hard squares of bean curd *(tau kwa)* are usually deep fried. Small cubes of dried deep-fried bean curd *(tau hoo tod)* are added to slow-cooked dishes and some soups. Pickled or fermented bean curd *(tau hoo yee)*, sold in jars and either red or white in color, is used in small amounts as a seasoning in Chinese-influenced dishes.

BEAN SPROUTS: Sprouted green mung peas *(tau ngork)* are eaten blanched in some salads and soups, or quickly stir-fried as a vegetable dish. They can be stored in a refrigerator for 2–3 days, if covered with water that is changed daily.

CARDAMOM *(luk grawan)*: Straw-colored pods

Horapa Basil *Kaprow Basil* *Manglak Basil* *Celery*

containing about 8–10 tiny black seeds with an intense fragrance.

CELERY (*ceun chai*): Thai celery is much smaller with thinner stems than the normal Western variety, and has a very intense flavor. The leaves and sometimes the stems are added to soups, some rice dishes and stir-fried vegetables. This type of celery is often obtainable in Asian speciality stores.

CHILI: Chilies are very popular and several varieties are commonly used. The large, finger-length green (unripe), red (ripe) or yellow chili (*prik chee*) is moderately hot; dried red chilies of this variety are ground to make chili flakes or chili powder. Tiny red, green or yellowy-orange bird's-eye chilies (*prik kee noo*) are used in soups, some liquid or curry-like dishes and sauces, and are extremely hot.

CHILI SAUCE (*saus prik*): Chilies mixed with water and seasoned with salt, sugar and vinegar are sold in bottles and jars, the best known overseas being the brand *Siracha*. Some sauces are sweeter than others, and go particularly well with either chicken or seafood (and are so labeled). Chili paste, known as *nam prik pow* is sometimes labeled "Burnt Chili Paste."

CHINESE FLAT CHIVES (*kui chai*): Rather like flat spring onions, these have a far more emphatic, garlicky flavor than regular Western chives.

CILANTRO (*pak chee*): The Thais must use cilantro, or fresh coriander, in all its forms, more than anyone else. The inimitable flavor of the fresh leaf garnishes countless dishes. The roots are pounded together with garlic and black pepper to provide a common basic seasoning, while dried coriander seeds are used to season a few dishes. There is no substitute for fresh cilantro; it can easily be grown from seed. Cilantro is available in most supermarkets; it is sold in bunches with the roots still attached.

CLOUD EAR FUNGUS (*hed hunu*): Also known as wood fungus, this is a shriveled grey-brown fungus which expands to at least four times its dried size after soaking in warm water. It is enjoyed for its chewy texture in some salads and stir-fried dishes.

COCONUT MILK (*nam maprow*): The flesh of mature coconuts is grated and squeezed without water to make **coconut cream**. To obtain **thick coconut milk**, about $\frac{1}{2}$ cup of water is added for each coconut, then squeezed and strained. **Thin

Chilies   *Cloud Ear fungus*   *Cilantro*   *Galangal*

coconut milk is obtained by adding 2 cups of water to the already squeezed coconut. Unless otherwise specified, "coconut milk" in this book is a combination of both thick and thin milks. Canned coconut milk, imported from Thailand or elsewhere, is inexpensive and often superior to the milk you can obtain from "fresh" coconuts sold in supermarkets.

CUMIN (*mellet yira*): This spice is sometimes added to curry pastes. The same Thai name is used for cumin, fennel and caraway, which are all similar in appearance, sometimes leading to confusion.

EGGPLANT (*ma-khue puang*): Several types of eggplant are used, ranging from the rather bitter pea-sized eggplant to slender green, white or purple-skinned varieties about 8–10 inches in length.

FISH SAUCE (*nam pla*): It's impossible to imagine Thai cuisine without this distinctive sauce, made from salted, fermented fish or prawns. Good quality *nam pla* is golden-brown in color and has a salty tang. It is used in much the same way as the Chinese use soy sauce.

GALANGAL (*kha*): A rhizome similar to ginger in appearance—and a member of the same family—this adds a wonderful flavor to many Thai dishes. Slices of dried galangal (sometimes sold under the Indonesian name *laos*) must be soaked in boiling water for about 30 minutes until softened. Jars of tender, sliced galangal packed in water are exported from Thailand and make an adequate substitute for the fresh root.

GARLIC (*kratiem*): Part of the common Thai combination of garlic, cilantro root and black pepper, large amounts of garlic are used in cooking. The size of garlic cloves is often much smaller in Southeast Asia than in Western countries, so use your discretion when following amounts given in the recipes.

GINGER (*king*): Use only fresh ginger in Thai cooking; dried powdered ginger has a completely different flavor. Young ginger, which is pale yellow with a pinkish tinge, is juicier than mature ginger, which has a light brown skin that should be scraped off before use.

JASMINE ESSENCE (*yod nam malee*): The heady perfume of fresh jasmine flowers, soaked overnight in water which is then used to make coconut milk, adds a unique fragrance to many Thai desserts and cakes. Substitute bottled jasmine essence.

JICAMA (*mun kaew*): This crunchy, mild tuber has

Kaffir Lime   *Krachai*   *Lemongrass*   *Straw Mushrooms*

a white interior and beige skin, which peels off easily. It is excellent eaten raw with a spicy dip, and can also be cooked.

KAFFIR LIME (*ma-grood*): This citrus fruit has a very knobby and intensely fragrant skin, but virtually no juice. The skin or rind is often grated and added to food, while the fragrant leaves are also used whole in soups and curries, or finely shredded and added to salads. Substitute dried leaves for fresh if fresh is unavailable. Dried rind can be reconstituted and substituted for fresh.

KRACHAI (*Kaemferia pandurata* or *Boesenbergia pandurata*): This unusual rhizome, which looks like a bunch of yellowish-brown fingers, is enjoyed for its mild flavor and crunchy texture. It is sometimes referred to as "lesser ginger." Dried *krachai* is a poor substitute; omit if the fresh variety is not available.

LEMONGRASS (*bai takrai*): A lemon-scented grass, which grows in clumps, this is very important in Thai cuisine. Each plant resembles a miniature leek. Use only the bottom 4–6 inches of the lemongrass, and if it is to be pounded or blended to a paste, discard several of the outer leaves and use only the tender center of the plant.

LILY BUDS, DRIED (*dok mai jeen*): Used in some vegetable dishes and soups of Chinese origin, these dried, golden-brown flowers are sometimes knotted for a more decorative appearance. Pinch off the hard bump at the end of each flower.

MINT (*bai saranee*): Popular in salads and the same plant that is used in Western countries.

MORNING GLORY: see **Water Spinach**

MUSHROOMS: Fresh mushrooms of several varieties are used, including delicate sheathed straw mushrooms (excellent in soups and vegetable dishes); button mushrooms, large, more bland oyster mushrooms and dried brownish-black Chinese mushrooms, which should be soaked in warm water to soften before use.

NOODLES: There are a number of varieties available, made from rice, wheat or mung-pea flour. The most popular varieties are **fresh flat rice-flour noodles** (*kwaytiaow*); **spaghetti-like fresh rice-flour noodles** (*kanom jeen*), which are similar to the *laksa* noodles of Malaysia and Singapore; **fresh egg noodles** (*ba mee*); **dried wheat-flour noodles**; **dried rice vermicelli** (*sen mee*), sometimes known as rice-stick noodles, and **cellophane noodles** or **bean threads** (*woon sen*), which are made from mung-pea flour

Mushrooms   Pandan Leaf   Shallots   Shrimp Paste

and are used in soups and salads.

OYSTER SAUCE (*nam man hoi*): Most brands of oyster sauce—often used in conjunction with fish sauce or soy sauce—contain monosodium glutamate and intensify the flavor of the dish to which they are added.

PALM SUGAR (*nam taan peep*): Made from the sap of either coconut palms or the *aren* (sugar palm) tree, palm sugar varies in color from gold to light brown. It is less sweet than cane sugar and has a distinctive flavor. If not available, use soft brown sugar or white cane sugar with a touch of maple syrup.

PANDAN LEAF (*bai toey hom*): A fragrant member of the pandanus or screwpine family, pandan leaf is used as a wrapping for seasoned morsels of chicken or pork rib. Look for fresh leaves at Southeast Asian produce stands. One-ounce packages of dried leaves labeled "Dried Bay-Tovy Leaves" are imported from Thailand, but fresh leaves are preferred.

PEPPERCORNS (*prik Thai*): Believed to have been the main source of heat before chilies arrived in Thailand, black pepper is still widely used. The whole peppercorns are crushed or ground only just before use for maximum flavor and freshness. Fresh green peppercorns are also added to some dishes.

PRAWNS, DRIED (*kung haeng*): Dried prawns as well as dried shrimp are used to season many dishes, particularly sauces. Dried shrimp, about $1/2$ inch long, retain their shells, heads and tails. They do not normally require soaking before use. Dried prawns, more commonly found overseas, are much thicker and usually longer, and are sold without their shells and heads. They should first be soaked in warm water for 5 minutes to soften.

RICE WINE: A splash of Chinese rice wine is often used to improve the flavor of dishes of Chinese origin. Dry sherry can be used as a substitute, although any Chinese grocery should stock this item.

SALTED CABBAGE (*pak kad khem*): Various types of heavily salted cabbage are used in some Thai-Chinese dishes. Soak in fresh water for at least 15 minutes to remove excess saltiness, repeating if necessary.

SALTED EGG (*kai khem*): Salted duck eggs are used as a side dish or pounded to make a sauce. The eggs should be boiled for about 10 minutes before being peeled.

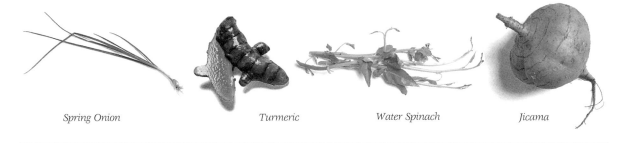

Spring Onion   *Turmeric*   *Water Spinach*   *Jicama*

SALTED FISH (*pla haeng*): Many varieties of freshwater fish are salted and sun dried; they are not soaked in water before using, but are either grilled or cut into fine slices and fried to a crisp.

SALTED SOY BEANS (*tau jiew*): Salty and with a distinctive tang, these are often lightly pounded before being used to season fish, noodle or some vegetable dishes. Varieties packed in China are sometimes confusingly labeled "Yellow Bean Sauce," while there are also brands which add sugar to already ground beans.

SESAME OIL (*naman ngaa*): Added to some dishes—usually at the last minute—for seasoning.

SHALLOTS (*hormlek*): Small round pinkish-purple shallots add a sweet oniony flavor to countless dishes, and are also sliced, deep fried and used as a garnish.

SHRIMP PASTE (*kapi*): Many different types of *kapi*, ranging in color from pink to blackish-brown, are available. The former is good for curry paste, the latter for making dipping sauces. Shrimp paste should be cooked before eating; if the recipe you are using does not call for it to be fried together with other ingredients, but just added to a dipping sauce where other ingredients are raw, either grill or dry fry the shrimp paste before pounding.

SHRIMP, DRIED: see **Prawns, Dried**

SOY SAUCE (*nam siew*): Light Chinese soy sauce and the dark black variety are both used in dishes of Chinese origin. Light soy is saltier, while dark soy adds flavor and a rich color to cooked dishes.

SPRING ONION (*ton horm*): Also called scallion or green onion, it is often cut to make a decorative tassel for garnishing food.

STAR ANISE (*poy kak bua*): A dried, dark brown star-shaped spice with a pungent aniseed flavor.

TAMARIND (*mak-kaam*): Dried tamarind pulp is soaked in water for 5–10 minutes, then squeezed and strained through a sieve to obtain the sour, fragrant juice. Discard any seeds and fibrous matter. If using already cleaned tamarind pulp or concentrate, reduce the amounts called for in these recipes.

TURMERIC (*kamin*): A member of the ginger family, this rhizome has a very rich yellow interior (which can stain clothing and plastic utensils) and a pleasant pungency that is absent in dried turmeric powder. Substitute $\frac{1}{2}$ teaspoon turmeric powder for $\frac{1}{2}$ inch fresh turmeric.

WATER CHESTNUT (*haew*): Although it is troublesome to peel away the dark brown skin of this crunchy tuber, it's well worth using fresh water chestnuts if you can find them. Their crisp texture and sweet flavor makes them popular in salads, some stir-fried vegetable dishes and even in desserts.

WATER SPINACH (*pak bung*): Also known in Thailand as morning glory (and as *kangkung* in Indonesia, Malaysia and Singapore), this aquatic plant is a delicious vegetable full of nutrition. Young shoots are often served as part of a mixed platter of raw vegetables for dipping into hot sauces, while the leaves and tender tips are also stir-fried. Discard the tough, hollow stems.

Part Three: The Recipes

*Recipes for curry pastes and dips precede those
for the main dishes, which begin on page 42*

Portions

In Thai homes, food is seldom served in individual portions, as rice and other side dishes are normally placed on the table for people to help themselves. It is thus difficult to estimate the exact number of portions each recipe will provide. As a general rule, however, the recipes in this book will serve 4–6 people as part of a meal with rice and three other dishes.

Seasoning Thai Food

The amount of chilies, fish sauce (which provides saltiness), sugar and lime juice given in the following recipes is a guide, not an absolute measure. Bear in mind that you can always increase the amount of seasonings when tasting the food just before serving, whereas if you overdo it in the initial stages, it's too late to reduce the seasoning later.

CURRY PASTES

Basic curry pastes (recipes start next page) can be stored in a covered glass jar in a refrigerator for 1 month or in a freezer for 3–4 months.

Ingredients

When a recipe lists a hard-to-find or unusual ingredient, see pages 30 to 35 for possible substitutes. If a substitute is not listed, look for the ingredient in your local Asian food market, or check the mail-order listings on page 130 for possible sources.

Time Estimates

Time estimates are for preparation only (excluding cooking) and are based on the assumption that a food processor or blender will be used.

- ⏱ *quick and very easy to prepare*

- ⏱⏱ *relatively easy; less than 15 minutes to prepare*

- ⏱⏱⏱ *takes more than 15 minutes to prepare*

***Opposite**:
Clock-wise from
bottom right:
Nam Prik Noom,
Nam Prik Gai
Kem, Kapi Kua,
Tau Jiew Lon,
Nam Prik Pla
Yaang, Nam Prik
Thai Orn, Nam
Prik Kapi.*

Nam Prik Gaeng Ped • *Red Curry Paste*

1 tablespoon coriander seeds
1 teaspoon cumin seed
13 dried bird's-eye chilies, cut, soaked in hot
   water for 15 minutes and deseeded
3 tablespoons finely chopped shallots
4 tablespoons finely chopped garlic
1 tablespoon finely chopped galangal
2 tablespoons finely sliced lemongrass
2 teaspoons finely chopped kaffir lime rind
1 tablespoon finely chopped cilantro root
20 black peppercorns
1 teaspoon shrimp paste

Dry fry the coriander and cumin seeds in a wok over low heat for about 5 minutes, then grind to a powder. Add the remaining ingredients, except the shrimp paste, and blend well. Add the ground spice mixture and shrimp paste and blend again to obtain about ¾ cup of fine-textured paste.

Nam Prik Pow • *Roasted Chili Paste*

2 cups vegetable oil
8 shallots, sliced
6 cloves garlic, sliced
1 cup dried prawns
½ cup small dried chilies
1 tablespoon palm sugar
3 tablespoons fish sauce
1½ tablespoons tamarind juice
¼–½ teaspoon salt

Heat the oil in a wok and fry the shallots and garlic until golden brown; remove from oil and drain. Add the dried prawns and chilies and fry until golden brown; remove from oil and drain.

In a food processor or blender, process the prawns, garlic, chilies, shallots and sugar until the mixture is well blended. Add the fish sauce, tamarind juice, salt and cooled oil from the wok and blend to obtain a finely textured paste.

Nam Prik Gaeng Kheow Wan • *Green Curry Paste*

1 tablespoon coriander seeds
1 teaspoon cumin seeds
15 green bird's-eye chilies
3 tablespoons finely chopped shallots
1 tablespoon finely chopped garlic
1 teaspoon finely chopped galangal
1 tablespoon finely sliced lemongrass
½ teaspoon finely chopped kaffir lime rind
1 teaspoon finely chopped cilantro root
5 black peppercorns
1 teaspoon salt
1 teaspoon shrimp paste

Dry fry the coriander and cumin seeds in a wok over low heat for about 5 minutes, then grind into a powder. Put the rest of the ingredients, except the shrimp paste, into a blender and blend to mix well. Add the spice seed mixture and shrimp paste and blend to obtain ½ cup of fine-textured paste.

Nam Prik Gaeng Mussaman • *Mussaman Curry Paste*

3 tablespoons finely chopped shallots
1 tablespoon finely chopped garlic
1 teaspoon finely chopped galangal
1 heaped tablespoon finely sliced lemongrass
2 cloves
1 tablespoon coriander seeds
1 teaspoon cumin seeds
5 black peppercorns
3 dried chilies, cut, soaked in hot water for

15 minutes and deseeded
1 teaspoon salt
1 teaspoon shrimp paste

Dry fry the shallots, garlic, galangal, lemongrass, cloves, coriander and cumin seeds in a wok over low heat for about 5 minutes, then grind into a powder. Add the rest of the ingredients, except the shrimp paste, and blend to mix well. Combine the blended mixture and the shrimp paste and blend again to obtain $\frac{1}{2}$ cup of fine-textured paste.

DIPS

Nam Prik Gai Kem • *Salted Egg Dip*

3 cloves garlic
3–4 red chilies
2 salted eggs, hard boiled
2 tablespoons lime juice
$\frac{1}{2}$ tablespoon fish sauce
1 teaspoon sugar

Pound garlic and chilies together. Add salted eggs and pound until well blended. Season with lime juice, fish sauce and sugar. Mix well. Serve with vegetables and fried or grilled fish.

Nam Prik Thai Orn • *Green Peppercorn Dip*

2 tablespoons fresh or bottled green peppercorns
3 cloves garlic
1 teaspoon sugar
$\frac{1}{2}$ tablespoon dried prawns
2–3 tablespoons lime juice
6 sour fruits such as green mango or green apple, sliced

If using bottled or canned green peppercorns, be sure to wash off brine thoroughly first. Pound in a mortar or blend the garlic and 1 tablespoon of peppercorns, then add sugar, dried prawns and lime juice. Mix well and add the remaining tablespoon of peppercorns. Stir until well mixed. Serve with sour fruit, vegetables and fried or grilled fish.

Nam Prik Kapi • *Shrimp Paste and Chili Dip*

1 tablespoon dried prawns or shrimp, soaked in water
5 cloves garlic
9 bird's-eye chilies
$1\frac{1}{2}$ tablespoons shrimp paste, roasted
1 teaspoon palm sugar
1 tablespoon fish sauce
2–3 tablespoons lime juice

Pound dried prawns, garlic and chilies together. Add shrimp paste, palm sugar, fish sauce and lime juice and mix well. Serve with fresh or cooked vegetables and fried or grilled fish.

Nam Prik Noom • *Green Chili Dip*

1 tablespoon chopped dried salted mackerel
4 tablespoons peanut or corn oil
10 large green chilies, chopped roughly
10 cloves garlic, chopped roughly
6 shallots, chopped roughly
1 tomato
2 tablespoons hot water
1 tablespoon chopped spring onion
1 tablespoon chopped cilantro leaves
Fish sauce, to taste (optional)

Fry the dried fish in the oil over medium heat for about 7–10 minutes and drain thoroughly.

Dry fry the chilies, garlic and shallots for about 8–10 minutes, stirring frequently, until fragrant. Pound lightly or blend briefly with the fish, then add the tomato. Pound or blend to break up the tomato, then add water, spring onion and cilantro.

Mix well. The sauce should be of a reasonably liquid consistency and a touch salty; if not, add more water or fish sauce as required.

This very hot dip is traditionally served with sticky rice as well as raw cabbage, sliced cucumbers, raw green beans and/or fried or roasted fish.

Nam Prik Pla Yaang • *Dip with Grilled Fish*

3-4 red bird's-eye chilies
1 dried chili, cut and soaked
3 cloves garlic, grilled in skin until blackened
2 shallots, grilled in skin until blackened
1 cup grilled, flaked fish
$\frac{1}{2}$ teaspoon shrimp paste, roasted
2 tablespoons lime juice
1 tablespoon fish sauce
1 teaspoon sugar
1 teaspoon kaffir lime juice

Pound bird's-eye chilies, then add dried chili, peeled garlic and shallots and continue pounding until ground into a fine paste. Add lime juice, fish sauce and sugar. Mix well and add kaffir lime juice. Serve with vegetables and grilled or fried fish.

Tau Jiew Lon • *Soy Bean and Coconut Milk Dip*

5 cups coconut milk
7 shallots, sliced or crushed
1 cup salted soy beans (*tau jiew*), rinsed
4 ounces shrimp, finely chopped (10 large)
4 ounces pork, finely chopped ($\frac{1}{2}$ cup)

1 tablespoon palm sugar
2 eggs
5 tablespoons finely shredded red chili
Fresh cilantro leaves to garnish

Bring coconut milk to a boil. Add shallots, salted soy beans, shrimp, pork and palm sugar. Mix well and stir in one egg at a time, stirring constantly. Cook until slightly reduced, then add chili shreds and garnish with cilantro leaves.

Kapi Kua • *Shrimp Paste and Coconut Milk Dip*

2 dried chilies, cut and soaked
5 shallots
5 stems lemongrass, finely sliced
3 slices galangal
3 tablespoons minced *krachai*
3 tablespoons shrimp paste, roasted
1 cup coarsely chopped smoked fish
4 cups coconut milk
1 tablespoon palm sugar
2 tablespoons fish sauce
5 red chilies

Pound dried chilies, shallots, lemongrass, galangal, *krachai* and shrimp paste with half the smoked fish until well mixed. Heat coconut milk and simmer until oil comes to the surface and the quantity has reduced.

Add the paste and continue cooking until fragrant. Add sugar, the rest of the fish, fish sauce and chilies and simmer until thick. Serve with grilled shrimp or fluffy crisp fish flakes in a pan and cook over low heat, stirring frequently, until the sauce has thickened and reduced. Cool to room temperature and garnish with cilantro leaves when serving.

Nam Prik Ong • *Pork and Tomato Chili Dip*

5 dried chilies, cut and soaked
1 teaspoon salt
1 tablespoon finely sliced galangal
3 tablespoons finely chopped onion
1 teaspoon shrimp paste
5 cloves garlic, left whole
3 ounces ground pork
1 cup sliced tomatoes
2 tablespoons oil
3 cloves garlic, chopped
1 whole cilantro plant
$^1\!/_2$ cup water
Fresh vegetables:
   cucumber, long
   beans, carrot,
   cabbage
Boiled vegetables: long
   beans, eggplant,
   pumpkin, cabbage

Pound the chilies, salt and galangal in a mortar or process in a blender. Add the onion, shrimp paste, whole garlic cloves and blend or pound thoroughly. Add the pork and continue processing. Finally, add the tomatoes and mix well.

Heat the oil in a wok, then gently fry the chopped garlic. When the garlic is fragrant, add pounded mixture and continue frying over low heat, stirring, until the ingredients take on a gloss. Add the water and continue cook-

ing, stirring frequently, until much of the water evaporates and the mixture becomes fairly thick.

Transfer to a bowl, sprinkle with chopped cilantro leaves and serve with fresh vegetables or boiled vegetables or both.

CHICKEN STOCK

5–6$^1\!/_2$ pounds chicken
   bones
6 quarts water
1$^1\!/_2$ cups chopped onion
1 cup chopped celery
1 tablespoon coriander
   seeds
1 teaspoon black
   peppercorns

Wash bones in cold water then put in a stockpot and cover with cold water. Bring rapidly to the boil, then drain and discard water. Cover bones with 6 quarts water and add all other ingredients. Simmer for 4 hours, removing the scum as it accumulates. Strain through cloth.

The stock can be put in 1-quart containers and frozen for up to 3 months. Home made chicken stock greatly improves the flavor of all recipes where stock is specified.

Nam Prik Ong, a spicy pork and tomato dip, surrounded by raw vegetables, salted duck egg and crisp pork skin.

MIENG KUM
Leaf-wrapped Savories

This is the sort of dish eaten at home, rather than at stalls or in restaurants. In Thailand, various edible tree leaves are used, but lettuce leaves make an acceptable substitute. ☉

1 head lettuce or bunch of edible leaves

Filling:

**5 tablespoons grated coconut, roasted in
    moderate oven until light brown
3 tablespoons finely diced shallots
3 tablespoons finely diced lime
3 tablespoons finely diced ginger
3 tablespoons small dried shrimp, chopped
3 tablespoons unsalted roasted peanuts
2 tablespoons chopped green bird's-eye chilies**

Sauce:

**1 tablespoon shrimp paste
$\frac{1}{2}$ tablespoon sliced galangal
$\frac{1}{2}$ tablespoon sliced shallots
2 tablespoons grated coconut
3 tablespoons chopped unsalted peanuts
2 tablespoons chopped dried shrimp
1 teaspoon sliced ginger
1 cup chopped palm sugar
$2\frac{1}{2}$ cups water**

Prepare the **sauce** first. Roast the shrimp paste, galangal and shallots until fragrant, then leave to cool. Place with the coconut, peanuts, shrimp and ginger in a blender or food processor and blend, or pound with a mortar and pestle until fine.

Transfer the mixture into a heavy-bottomed pan with the sugar and water, mix well and bring to a boil. Simmer until it is reduced to about 1 cup, then let it cool.

To serve, pour the sauce into a serving bowl and arrange all the ingredients in separate piles on small bowls. To eat, take a lettuce leaf, place a small amount of each of the filling ingredients in the middle, top with a spoonful of sauce and fold up into a little package.

KRATHONG THONG
Patty Shells with Minced Chicken

The delicate crisp shells used for this snack are made using a special brass mold. Thin short-crust pastry shells or even *vol-au-vent* cases can be used instead. ☉ ☉

Patty Shells:
- $^1/_2$ **cup rice flour**
- **6 tablespoons white flour**
- **4 tablespoons thin coconut milk**
- **2 tablespoons tapioca starch**
- **1 egg yolk**
- $^1/_4$ **teaspoon sugar**
- $^1/_4$ **teaspoon salt**
- $^1/_4$ **teaspoon baking soda**
- **4 cups peanut or corn oil**

Filling:
- **2 tablespoons peanut or corn oil**
- **4 tablespoons finely diced onion**
- **2 cups cooked chicken or pork, finely chopped**
- $^1/_4$ **cup corn kernels**
- **2 tablespoons finely diced carrot**
- **2 tablespoons sugar**
- $^1/_4$ **teaspoon black soy sauce**
- $^1/_2$ **teaspoon salt**
- $^1/_2$ **teaspoon white pepper**
- **Cilantro leaves for garnish**
- **1 red chili, finely sliced**

Opposite:
Krathong Thong (left) and Tong Geon Yong (right). Recipe for Tong Geon Yong is on page 46.

Make the **patty shells** first by mixing all ingredients, except oil, together in a bowl. Heat the oil, then dip the *krathong* mold in the oil to heat up. Dip the mold into the batter and plunge back into oil. Fry for about 5 minutes until light brown, then shake to remove the cup from the mold. Place on paper towels to drain. Repeat to make 20–25 cups.

Now make the **filling**. Put the oil in a hot wok and stir fry onion and pork or chicken for 2 minutes. Add the rest of the ingredients and fry for about 3 minutes until the vegetables are fairly soft. Leave them to cool, then divide the filling among the patty shells. Garnish with cilantro leaves and slices of fresh red chili.

Helpful hint: If using a *krathong* mold, be sure that it is very hot before plunging it into the batter; the batter must adhere to the mold as you put it back into the oil to cook.

TONG GEON YONG & SAKUNA CHOMSUAN

Pork and Shrimp Rolls & Shrimp with Sweet and Sour Sauce

PORK AND SHRIMP ROLLS

The Chinese influence on this dish is evident in the use of dried bean curd skin. The filling can be made in advance and the rolls assembled just before frying. ☻

4 ounces shrimp or prawns, finely chopped
4 ounces pork, finely chopped
1 tablespoon light soy sauce
1 teaspoon each of cilantro root, garlic and peppercorn, pounded together
Squares of dried bean curd skin (available in Asian food markets)
4 cups corn oil

Opposite:
*Sakuna
Chomsuan.
Photograph of
Tong Geon Yong
is on page 45.*

Mix shrimp and pork with soy sauce and the pounded cilantro root, garlic and peppercorn. Wipe sheets of dried bean curd skin with a moist cloth and cut into 4-inch by 6-inch squares. Put in a spoonful of the filling and roll up like a cigar.

Alternatively, cut circles about 3 inches in diameter and place a little filling in the center. Squeeze in the sides to make a bundle and tie with a strip of spring onion.

Deep fry the rolls in hot oil over medium heat until golden brown. Serve with soy sauce or plum sauce.

SHRIMP WITH SWEET AND SOUR SAUCE

A simple but always popular appetizer. The shrimp can be prepared in advance and deep fried just before serving. Use any commercial brand of sweet and sour sauce for dipping. ☻

1 pound large shrimp
2 eggs, lightly beaten
4 cups fine bread crumbs
Cooking oil for deep frying

Peel the shrimp, discard the heads but leave on the tail sections. Slit down the back of each shrimp, remove the intestinal tract and flatten the shrimp into a butterfly shape by pressing gently with the hand. Dip the shrimp in the egg and bread crumbs. Deep fry until golden and serve with sweet and sour sauce.

CHOR LADDA

Dumplings with Minced Pork and Shrimp

The brilliant blue color of these dumplings is obtained by soaking a blue flower (*anchun*), although commercial food coloring can be substituted. ☉☉

Filling:
$^1/_2$ cup roasted unsalted peanuts, chopped
$^1/_2$ teaspoon salt
2 tablespoons sugar
4 ounces minced pork ($^1/_2$ cup)
4 ounces minced shrimp (10 large)
4 ounces chopped salted radish (1 cup)
2 tablespoons cooking oil

Dumplings:
$^1/_4$ cup tapioca starch
About 2 tablespoons dried *anchun* flowers or
   1 teaspoon blue food coloring
2 cups rice flour
$^1/_4$ cup coconut milk
2 tablespoons cooking oil
$^1/_4$ cup water
Banana leaf or aluminum foil
$^1/_2$ cup coconut cream

Stir fry all the **filling** ingredients together in oil until cooked and let cool.

Make the **dumplings** by mixing all ingredients together. Cook over low heat, stirring constantly, until the mixture turns into an elastic dough. Cover with plastic wrap while making the individual dumplings to prevent the dough from drying out.

Pinch off a small ball of dough and flatten into a circle about $2^1/_2$ inches in diameter. Place a teaspoonful of stuffing in the center of the dough and pinch edges together to enclose. Use special tongs or pinch to give the dumplings a flower shape. Place on an oiled banana leaf or aluminum foil and put about 1 teaspoon of coconut cream over the top of each dumpling to prevent it from drying out.

Steam dumplings for 8 minutes until cooked. Serve warm on a bed of crisp-fried golden garlic and top with coconut cream.

Helpful hint: In Thailand, a pair of miniature tongs with serrations on the inside is used to pinch the dough to create the "petals." Failing such an esoteric utensil, use your fingers to pinch the dough into a decorative shape.

TOM YAM GOONG

Spicy Shrimp Soup with Lemongrass

One of the best known Thai dishes abroad, this is hot, sour and fragrant, an ideal accompaniment to other Thai dishes and rice. ✷ ✷

3 cups chicken stock (page 41)
3 kaffir lime leaves
2 inches galangal
3 stems lemongrass
5–6 medium to large shrimp or prawns
5 ounces straw mushrooms
5 green and red bird's-eye chilies
4 tablespoons lime juice, or to taste
$^1/_2$ tablespoon fish sauce, or to taste
Handful fresh cilantro leaves

Bring the stock to a boil, add lemongrass, galangal and kaffir lime, then add the shrimp and mushrooms. Simmer for 3–4 minutes until the shrimp are cooked, then add chilies, lime juice and fish sauce. Taste and add more lime or fish sauce if needed; the soup should be spicy-sour and a little salty. Serve garnished with fresh cilantro.

Helpful hints: Do not overcook the shrimp or they will become tough. Be sure to use homemade chicken stock for the best possible flavor.

POH TAEK

Spicy Seafood Soup

Thailand's abundance of seafood makes mixed seafood dishes common. The wonderful flavor of this soup is enhanced by the use of lemon-scented herbs and galangal. 🕐 🕐

6 cups chicken stock (page 41)
6 ounces seabass or other fish, cleaned and cut into 6 pieces
5 large shrimp or prawns
1 blue crab, cleaned, back shell discarded and cut into 6 pieces
6 mussels in their shells, cleaned well
6 ounces squid, cleaned and cut into $^3/_4$-inch slices
2 stems lemongrass, cut into $^1/_4$-inch lengths
3 inches galangal, sliced
3 kaffir lime leaves
Handful basil (*horapa*) leaves
8 green bird's-eye chilies, crushed lightly
5 dried red chilies, dry-fried lightly
$^1/_4$ teaspoon palm sugar
3 tablespoons fish sauce, or to taste
1 tablespoon lemon juice, or to taste

Bring chicken stock to a boil and add all the fish and seafood. Add the lemongrass, galangal and lime leaf and return to a boil. Add all remaining ingredients and cook for 2 more minutes, then remove from the heat. Taste and add fish sauce and lemon juice to taste.

Serve in bowls accompanied by rice, fish sauce and lemon juice.

TOM KHA GAI

Spicy Chicken Soup with Coconut Milk

A delightful soup, creamy with coconut milk and fragrant with the elusive flavor of galangal. Reduce the amount of chilies if you don't want the soup to be too spicy. ☯ ☯

 1 cup chicken stock (page 41)
 2 stems lemongrass
 2 inches galangal
 3 kaffir lime leaves, torn into small pieces
 $^3/_4$ pound chicken
 4 ounces straw mushrooms
 1 teaspoon salt
 4 tablespoons lime juice
 3 tablespoons fish sauce
 $^1/_2$ teaspoon sugar
 4 cups coconut milk
 6 red bird's-eye chilies, bruised

Place the stock in a pot, add the lemongrass, galangal and kaffir lime leaves. Bring to a boil over medium heat. Add the chicken, mushrooms, salt, lime juice, fish sauce and sugar. Cook slowly, uncovered, for 10 minutes, then add coconut milk and chilies. Bring almost to a boil, stirring frequently, then remove from heat and serve.

Helpful hint: Cook gently to prevent the coconut milk from separating.

GAENG JUED WOON SEN & GAENG NOPPAKAO
Clear Soup with Cellophane Noodles & Mixed Vegetable Soup

CLEAR SOUP WITH CELLOPHANE NOODLES

Gaeng jued (literally "plain soup") is clear and mild, serving as a contrast to accompanying dishes that are either oily or spicy. ⏲⏲

Opposite:
Gaeng Noppakao (left) and Gaeng Jued Woon Sen (right).

10 ounces ground pork (1 cup)
1/2 teaspoon light soy sauce
1/4 teaspoon white pepper
4 cups chicken stock (page 41)
7 white peppercorns, crushed
5 cloves garlic, crushed
8 ounces cellophane noodles, soaked in water
1 teaspoon fish sauce
1/4 teaspoon sugar
3 spring onions, cut into 1/2-inch pieces
2 tablespoons chopped cilantro leaves

Mix the pork, soy sauce and white pepper together well and form into small meatballs.

Heat the chicken stock, add the crushed peppercorns and garlic and bring to the boil. Place the meat balls in the boiling stock and then add the noodles, fish sauce and sugar. Simmer until the meatballs are cooked. Add the spring onion and cilantro and remove from the heat immediately.

Serve accompanied by rice.

Helpful hint: Cellophane or clear noodles need to be soaked in warm water for about 5 minutes to soften and swell.

MIXED VEGETABLE SOUP

This is not so much a soup in the Western sense, but vegetables seasoned with a little pork, chicken and shrimp simmered in seasoned stock. ⏲⏲

5 cups mixed vegetables, such as summer squash or zucchini, pumpkin, straw mushrooms, baby corn, green beans, cut into bite sizes
1/4 pound lean pork, very thinly sliced
1/4 pound chicken, very thinly sliced
1/4 pound shrimp, peeled but tails left on
4 cups chicken stock (page 41)
2 tablespoons fish sauce
1 cup lemon basil (*manglak*) leaves

Seasoning:

10 black peppercorns
1 tablespoon shrimp paste
10 shallots
1/2 cup dried prawns or shrimp

Place **seasoning** ingredients in a mortar or blender and pound or blend until fine.

Add this mixture to chicken stock and bring to a boil, stirring to prevent sticking. Add the vegetables, pork, chicken and shrimp and simmer until just cooked. Season to taste with fish sauce or salt, then remove from heat. Add basil and serve.

GAENG SOM

Sour Soup with Vegetables and Shrimp

Sour but fragrant tamarind juice adds a special touch to this relatively mild soup, which is chock-full of vegetables and flavored with pounded shrimp or fish. As with other types of Gaeng, this has very little liquid. 🕐🕐

$^3/_4$ **pound shrimp or fish fillets**
$^1/_4$ **pound straw mushrooms**
1 large white radish, sliced
$^1/_2$ **cup sliced green papaya**
$^1/_2$ **cup green beans, cut in 1-inch pieces**
$^2/_3$ **cup cauliflower, broken into florets**
1 cup Chinese white cabbage, cut in
   1-inch pieces
4 tablespoons tamarind juice
1 tablespoon palm sugar
1 teaspoon salt

Spice Paste:
3 dried chilies, soaked until soft
2 teaspoons finely chopped *krachai* (optional)
2 teaspoons finely chopped garlic
2 teaspoons finely chopped shallots

Simmer the shrimp or fish fillets in just enough water to cover until cooked. Allow to cool in the stock, then peel the shrimp or remove any bones from the fish. Measure 1 cup of stock and set aside.

Pound or process the fish or shrimp until well mashed and set aside. Pound or blend the spice paste ingredients, then put in a pan with the reserved stock, shrimp or fish and vegetables. Bring to a boil and simmer until just cooked. Add the tamarind juice, sugar and salt to taste.

Helpful hint: Any combination of vegetables can be used; suggested alternatives include chayote, any other type of summer squash or zucchini, eggplant, green cabbage and button mushrooms.

PAD THAI GOONG SOD
Fried Rice Noodles with Shrimp

Dried rice-flour vermicelli is used for this dish, one of the dozens of noodle creations found in Thailand. The pickled white radish is available in cans, usually packed in China. ☻ ☻

¹/₂ cup oil
1 tablespoon chopped garlic
1 tablespoon chopped shallots
10 ounces dried rice-flour vermicelli, soaked in warm water to soften
1 tablespoon chopped pickled white radish
1 cake hard bean curd
1 teaspoon ground dried chilies
4 tablespoons sugar
3 tablespoons fish sauce
4 tablespoons tamarind juice
3 eggs
1 pound bean sprouts
Bunch of Chinese flat chives
¹/₂ cup ground roasted peanuts
¹/₂ banana blossom, simmered until tender (optional)
4 pieces large or jumbo shrimp, grilled, about 3–4 ounces each

Heat 3 tablespoons oil in a wok and sauté garlic and shallots. Add the noodles and fry, turning constantly to prevent sticking. Remove noodles and set aside.

Put another 3 tablespoons of oil into pan, and when hot, add the pickled white radish, bean curd and dried chilies. Stir fry for 2–3 minutes and then return the noodles. Add sugar, fish sauce and tamarind juice, mix thoroughly and set aside on a plate.

Put another 2 tablespoons of oil into the pan and when hot, break 3 eggs into pan and scramble, spreading the eggs in a thin layer over the pan. When set, return noodles and mix together. Add half the bean sprouts and Chinese flat chives. Mix together thoroughly, then sprinkle with ground peanuts. Season with sugar, fish sauce and tamarind juice.

Serve garnished with the remaining bean sprouts and Chinese flat chives, the banana blossom and grilled shrimp.

Helpful hint: Fried noodles require a lot of oil; however, it is possible to use a minimum amount by adding small amounts from time to time to keep the noodles from drying out instead of adding all the oil at once.

KWAYTIAOW PAD KEEMAO THALAY

Fresh Rice-flour Noodles with Seafood and Basil

Fresh *kwaytiaow* or flat rice-flour noodles, Chinese in origin, are now enthusiastically enjoyed in most parts of Thailand. They are served either in soups or stir fried with savory ingredients. This version of fried *kwaytiaow* is understandably popular in coastal areas where a wide variety of seafood is available. 🕐 🕐

1 pound mixed seafood, such as squid, prawns, fish, steamed clams or mussels
3 tablespoons crushed garlic
Scant $^1/_2$ cup oil
2 tablespoons light soy sauce
1 pound fresh rice-flour noodles
3 tablespoons fish sauce
A few basil leaves (*horapa*)
3 red chilies, roughly chopped
White pepper to taste

Cut seafood into pieces. Fry the garlic in 4 tablespoons oil until golden brown, then discard garlic. Put in the seafood and sauté for a few minutes in the same oil. Drain and put to one side.

Stir fry the noodles with soy sauce in the remaining oil for 2–3 minutes, then add the cooked seafood. Mix well and add fish sauce, basil leaves and chilies. Stir, sprinkle with white pepper to taste and cook for a minute more.

Helpful hint: If fresh rice-flour noodles are not available, substitute $^3/_4$ pound dried rice noodles, soaked in warm water to soften.

KHAO SOI
Northern-style Chicken Noodle Soup

This Burmese-influenced dish, with a curry-like gravy bathing chicken and noodles, is very popular at lunch time in Chiang Mai and other northern towns. ⊘ ⊘

6 cups coconut milk
10 ounces boneless skinned chicken breasts,
  cut lengthwise into $1/2$-inch slices
1 tablespoon light soy sauce
1 tablespoon black soy sauce
2 teaspoons salt
12 ounces dried egg noodles
Peanut or corn oil for frying

Chili Paste:

4 dried chilies, chopped roughly
1 tablespoon chopped shallots
2 teaspooons sliced ginger
1 teaspoon coriander seeds
$1/2$ teaspoon turmeric powder

Accompaniments:

2 tablespoons sliced shallots
$1/4$ cup chopped pickled cabbage
1 tablespoon ground dried chilies

Make the **chili paste** first by dry-roasting all ingredients for about 8–10 minutes until fragrant, then pound or process until fine.

Heat 1 cup of coconut milk, add the chili paste and cook for 2 minutes, then add the chicken and soy sauces. Stir fry for 3 minutes, then add the rest of the coconut milk and bring to a boil. Simmer for 3 minutes, then add the salt and remove from the heat.

Fry 4 ounces of the noodles in hot oil until crisp. Remove and drain well. Boil the rest of the noodles in water until cooked but still lightly firm, then drain.

Place the boiled noodles in serving bowls and pour the chicken and coconut mixture on top. Garnish with the fried noodles. Accompany with bowls of sliced shallots, chopped pickled cabbage and ground chili, allowing each person to add a little according to taste.

KWAYTIAOW NUEA SAB

Fresh Rice-flour Noodles with Minced Beef

This is another version of the popular Chinese *kwaytiaow* noodles (see page 62). 🕐 🕐

1 teaspoon chopped garlic
Scant $^1/_2$ cup oil
1 pound fresh flat rice-flour noodles
$^1/_2$ tablespoon black soy sauce
6 lettuce leaves
2 tablespoons finely chopped shallots
10 ounces finely minced beef
$^1/_2$ cup water
3 teaspoons light soy sauce
1 teaspoon cornstarch, blended with 2
   tablespoons water
4–6 quail eggs, hard-boiled and peeled
   (optional)
Salt and pepper to taste

Brown the garlic in 6 tablespoons oil, then add the noodles and sauté for 1–2 minutes, adding the black soy sauce. Pour the noodles over the lettuce leaves.

Brown the shallots in the rest of the oil. Add the meat, water, light soy sauce and stir well. When the sauce begins to boil, stir in the blended cornstarch and quail eggs (if using). Season to taste with salt and pepper. Simmer for a couple of minutes until the sauce thickens and clears, then pour the mixture over the noodles and serve.

Helpful Hint: If fresh rice-flour noodles are unavailable, substitute $^3/_4$ pound dried rice noodles, soaked in warm water to soften.

KANOM JEEN NAM YAA
Rice Noodles with Fish Curry Sauce

An excellent and tasty light meal, using the round fresh rice-flour noodles known as *kanom jeen*. Because of their length, *kanom jeen* are commonly served at family ceremonies, including marriages and birthdays; never broken until served, they signify long life. If fresh rice-flour noodles are not available, use fresh pasta such as the fine angel-hair variety. ☺☺☺

Sauce:

7 shallots, coarsely chopped
2 cloves garlic
2 slices galangal
2 tablespoons sliced lemongrass
1 cup minced *krachai* (optional)
3 dried chilies, seeds removed
1 teaspoon salt
1 teaspoon shrimp paste
1 cup water

Stock:

1 small, well-flavored fish (about $1/2$ pound)
$4^1/_2$ cups coconut milk
$1/_2$ cup coconut cream
2–3 tablespoons fish sauce

Accompaniments:

2 pounds fresh rice noodles (*kanom jeen*) or fresh angel-hair pasta
2 hard-boiled eggs, peeled and cut into quarters
$1/_2$ cup sliced cabbage
$1/_2$ cup sliced cucumber
$1/_2$ cup blanched bean sprouts
1 small bunch lemon basil (*manglak*)
1 tablespoon ground dried chilies

Place all **sauce** ingredients in a pot and simmer over low heat until soft. Remove from heat, cool, place in mortar or blender and pound or blend until fine.

Prepare the **stock** next. Wash and clean the fish, removing head, and simmer in just enough water to cover until soft. Drain and save the water in which the fish was boiled. Remove the meat from the fish, add to the chili paste in the mortar or blender and pound or blend to mix thoroughly.

Put the sauce into a pot and add the coconut milk. Bring to a boil, then add the fish broth and fish sauce. Simmer, stirring regularly to prevent sticking, until the sauce has thickened and the surface glistens bright red. Add the coconut cream and remove from heat.

Arrange a portion of the rice noodles and a little of each of the accompaniments in individual bowls. Spoon the sauce over just before serving.

KHAO YAM PAK TAI
Southern-style Rice Salad

This is a popular way of using leftover rice and makes an ideal light luncheon dish. The seasonings added to the rice can be varied according to taste and availability; not all ingredients used in the following recipe are shown in the photograph opposite. ◑ ◑

> 2 cups cold cooked rice
> 2 cups grated coconut, browned in oven for
>   5–8 minutes
> 1 small pomelo or grapefruit, sectioned
> 1 small green mango, shredded (optional)
> ½ cup dried shrimp, chopped
> ½ cup bean sprouts
> ½ cup finely sliced lemongrass
> ¼ cup sliced green beans
> 1 egg, beaten, cooked into an omelet and
>   shredded
> 2 dried red chilies, pounded
> 1 tablespoon very finely shredded kaffir
>   lime leaf
> 1 tablespoon chopped fresh coriander
> 4 ounces cooked prawns for garnish (optional)
> lime wedges

Sauce:

> 1 cup water
> 2 tablespoons chopped anchovies in brine
> 1 tablespoon chopped palm sugar
> 2 kaffir lime leaves, torn into small pieces
> ½ inch lemongrass, very finely sliced

Put all the **sauce** ingredients in pan, bring to a boil and simmer for 5 minutes. Remove from heat, strain and set aside.

Place the rice in small bowls, each holding about half a cup. Press down then invert onto a large serving platter. Arrange the rest of raw ingredients around the edge of rice in separate piles.

To eat, spoon some rice onto individual plates and take a little of each ingredient to mix with the rice according to taste. Spoon the sauce over the top.

Helpful hints: Canned anchovies packed in Europe make an acceptable substitute for the preserved Thai variety. If the very fine dried shrimp used in Thailand are not available, substitute with packaged fish floss.

SOM TAM THAI
Green Papaya Salad

Originally an Isan dish from the northeast, this excellent salad is now prepared by roadside hawkers all over the country. Som Tam captures the essential flavors of Thailand: chili hot, redolent with garlic and fish sauce and sour with lime juice. The basic ingredient, unripe papaya, contrasts in texture with raw beans and peanuts. ☉ ☉

  10 ounces unripe green papaya, peeled and cut
       in very fine matchsticks
  7 green bird's-eye chilies
  5 cloves garlic
  2 ounces long beans, cut in $1/2$-inch pieces
       ($1/2$ cup)
  2 tablespoons unsalted roasted peanuts
  1 tablespoon dried shrimp
  6 cherry tomatoes, quartered, or 1 large
       tomato, in wedges
  3 tablespoons lime juice
  1 tablespoon chopped palm sugar
  1 tablespoon fish sauce

Take a little of the papaya, chilies and garlic and pound roughly in a mortar and pestle or process very briefly in a blender. Set aside in a bowl and repeat until all the papaya, chilies and garlic are used.

Stir in the beans, peanuts, dried shrimp and tomato, mix well and add the seasonings.

Serve accompanied by raw vegetables (cabbage, water spinach or morning glory) and sprigs of basil; for a complete meal, add glutinous rice and roasted chicken.

Helpful hints: If using dried prawns rather than dried shrimp, soak in warm water for 5 minutes then chop coarsely. Prepare the salad immediately before eating, otherwise the papaya will lose its firm texture.

YAM SOM-O

Spicy Pomelo Salad

Large round pomelos, the forerunner to grapefruit, are generally full of sweet juice, and are eaten as a fruit as well as mixed with sour, spicy ingredients to make a salad. A favorite Thai snack is to just dip segments of pomelo into whatever sauce or Prik happens to be available. This salad goes well with rice and other cooked dishes. ⊘

1 pomelo or 2 grapefruit
2 tablespoons lime juice
1 tablespoon fish sauce
1 tablespoon sugar
$\frac{1}{3}$ pound cooked shrimp
8 ounces cooked chicken breast, shredded
   (2 cups)
2 tablespoons grated fresh or dried coconut
$\frac{1}{2}$ cup coconut cream
1 tablespoon dried shrimp, finely chopped

Peel the pomelo and shred the flesh (if using grapefruit, peel and section). Place the lime juice, fish sauce and sugar in a bowl and stir to mix. Then add the shrimp, chicken, grated coconut and coconut cream and continue stirring until blended. Add the pomelo and toss to coat thoroughly.

Transfer to serving plate, sprinkle with dried shrimp and serve.

Helpful hint: If dried shrimp are not available, use fish floss or omit altogether.

PLA NUEA MAKREUA ORN

Beef Salad with Eggplant

Although uncooked beef can be used for this salad, it is also an ideal way to use up any leftover roast or grilled beef. 🕐 🕐

- **3 small round green eggplant or 1 long thin eggplant**
- **3 tablespoons oil**
- **10 ounces uncooked or cooked beef fillet, sliced**
- **1 tablespoon sliced shallots**
- **5 green bird's-eye chilies, coarsely chopped**
- **2 tablespoons lime juice**
- **1 tablespoon fish sauce**
- **$1/4$ teaspoon sugar**

Cut the eggplant into $1/2$-inch slices and fry until cooked. Put into a bowl.

If using uncooked beef, sauté in a frying pan in a little oil over high heat until done. Combine the beef with the eggplant and the remaining ingredients and mix well.

Serve at room temperature with white rice.

PAD PAK RUAM MIT
Fried Mixed Vegetables

This method of cooking vegetables can be used for individual vegetables, such as kale or broccoli, or almost any combination of vegetables depending on availability and your preference. ⏱

$^1\!/_2$ cup snow peas
2 cups chopped young kale
$^3\!/_4$ cup chopped cabbage
$^3\!/_4$ cup chopped broccoli
$^1\!/_2$ cup chopped cauliflower
$^3\!/_4$ cup sliced mushrooms
$^1\!/_2$ cup baby sweet corn
$^1\!/_4$ cup peanut or corn oil
3 tablespoons finely chopped garlic
$^1\!/_2$ cup chicken stock (page 41)
4 tablespoons oyster sauce
1 tablespoon light soy sauce
$^1\!/_4$ teaspoon black soy sauce
$^1\!/_2$ teaspoon ground white pepper

Cut or slice the vegetables into bite-sized pieces and mix together in a bowl. Plunge them into boiling water for a few seconds to blanch, then drain and set aside.

Heat a wok until lightly smoking and add the oil. When hot, add the garlic and stir well. Add the vegetables and chicken stock all at once and stir fry for about 3–4 minutes until just cooked; the vegetables should still be slightly crisp. Add the oyster sauce and soy sauces, then sprinkle with pepper. Mix well and cook for 1 minute. Serve accompanied by rice.

Helpful hint: Use maximum heat to stir fry the vegetables to ensure the right texture and flavor.

KANA MOO GROB

Kale with Crispy Pork

Vegetables are frequently cooked with a little meat, poultry or seafood to add flavor and a contrasting texture. Kale, known in Thailand by its Chinese name, *kai lan*, is enjoyed for its firm stems. If this vegetable is not available, try using broccoli stems instead. 🕐🕐

2 pounds kale or 1 pound broccoli stems
3 tablespoons oil
1 tablespoon finely chopped garlic
10 ounces crispy pork, diced (about 4 cups)
4 tablespoons oyster sauce
$^1/_4$ teaspoon salt
$^1/_4$ teaspoon ground white pepper
1 teaspoon sugar
1 cup chicken stock (page 41)

Discard the leaves and tough bottom part of the kale stems. Peel the skin off the tender stems and discard. Cut stems in 2-inch to 3-inch lengths.

Heat the oil in a wok. When it is very hot, fry the garlic until fragrant, then add the kale and crispy pork. Stir to mix well, and then add all the seasonings and stock. Mix well, heat through and then serve immediately.

Helpful hints: Roasted pork with a layer of meat, a thin layer of fat and crisp, golden-brown skin, contrasts beautifully in taste and texture with the vegetable. Although unconventional, thick slices of crisp fried bacon make an excellent substitute. Two pounds of bacon, cooked, will yield approximately 10 ounces of cooked meat.

PLA MUK TOD & CHU CHEE GOONG LAI

Fried Squid with Garlic & Sautéed Shrimp with Chili

FRIED SQUID WITH GARLIC & BLACK PEPPER

Despite its simplicity and speed of preparation, this is an absolutely delicious way of cooking squid. ⏱

1¼ pounds fresh squid
2 tablespoons oil
½ cup chopped garlic
1 teaspoon black peppercorns, crushed
2 tablespoons oyster sauce
2 tablespoons light soy sauce
1 teaspoon sugar
Cilantro leaves to garnish

Opposite:
*Chu Chee Goong
Lai (above) and
Pla Muk Tod
(below).*

Remove the tentacles from the squid and cut out the hard beaky portion. Remove the skin from the body of the squid, clean inside and cut into bite-sized pieces. Dry thoroughly and set aside.

Put the oil in a wok over medium heat. Fry the garlic until golden-brown, then add the squid and its tentacles, together with the seasonings. Cook for a couple of minutes until the squid turns white. Serve hot sprinkled with cilantro leaves.

Helpful hint: Be sure to use fresh and not frozen squid, as the latter exudes water when cooked, making it stew rather than fry.

SAUTÉED SHRIMP WITH CHILI

A curry-like dish where the prawns are cooked in a spicy coconut-milk gravy, this gains additional flavor from the addition of basil. Although large tiger shrimp (about 6 per pound) are normally used, smaller ones can be substituted. ⏱⏱

12 ounces jumbo tiger shrimp
½ cup coconut cream
2 tablespoons red curry paste (page 38)
2½ cups coconut milk
3 tablespoons fish sauce
2 tablespoons chopped palm sugar
2 shredded kaffir lime leaves
Basil (*horapa*) or cilantro leaves to garnish
3 red chilies, cut in fine lengthwise strips

Peel the shrimp, discarding the head and tail. Cut shrimp down the back and remove the intestinal tract.

Heat the coconut cream, add the curry paste and cook, stirring, until fragrant. Bring the coconut milk to a boil, then add the shrimp. Simmer for 15 minutes until shrimp are cooked. Season to taste with fish sauce and palm sugar.

Place shrimp on a serving platter garnished with shreds of kaffir lime leaves, basil and chilies.

GOONG POW

Charcoal-grilled Prawns with Sweet Sauce

The fragrance of seafood grilling over charcoal is irresistible. In Thailand, this dish is made with huge fresh-water prawns. Small crayfish could be used instead. ⏱

**3 large fresh-water prawns or small crayfish
Foil or banana leaf**

Sauce:
**$^1\!/_3$ cup water
1 tablespoon sugar
$^1\!/_2$ teaspoon salt
$1^1\!/_2$ tablespoons chopped garlic
$^1\!/_2$ tablespoon chopped chilies
1 teaspoon chopped fresh cilantro
2 tablespoons lime juice**

Prepare the **sauce** first. Heat the water and sugar in a pan over low heat, stirring until the sugar has dissolved. Turn off the heat, add the salt and stir well. Remove from heat and allow to cool, then add the remaining ingredients and mix thoroughly.

Clean the crayfish or prawns and wrap each securely in foil or banana leaf. Grill over a hot charcoal fire for about 12 minutes. Serve with sauce.

POO OB WOON SEN

Casseroled Crabs with Cellophane Noodles

Food cooked in a clay pot is Chinese in origin. One popular adaptation in Thailand uses either crab claws or whole crabs cut into serving pieces. Although slices of pork fat are normally used, bacon improves the flavor of an already tasty dish. ☺ ☺

2 slices lean bacon, cut into 1-inch pieces
2 whole crabs, shelled, or 1 pound crab claws
2 cilantro roots, cut in half
2 inches ginger, pounded or chopped finely
3–4 cloves garlic, chopped
1 tablespoon white peppercorns, crushed
8 ounces cellophane noodles (*woon sen*) soaked
   in cold water for 5 minutes
1 teaspoon butter
3 tablespoons black soy sauce
$^1/_4$ cup chopped cilantro leaves and stems
2 spring onions, cut in $1^1/_2$-inch lengths

Stock:

2 cups chicken stock (page 41)
2 tablespoons oyster sauce
2 tablespoons black soy sauce
$^1/_2$ tablespoon sesame oil
1 teaspoon brandy or whisky
$^1/_2$ teaspoon sugar

Place all the **stock** ingredients in a pan, bring to a boil and simmer for 5 minutes. Leave to cool.

Take a heat-proof casserole dish and place the bacon over the base. Put in the crab, cilantro root, ginger, garlic and peppercorns. Place the noodles over the top, then add the butter, soy sauce and soup stock.

Cover and bring to a boil. Simmer for 5 minutes. Mix well with tongs and add the cilantro and spring onions. Cover and simmer for about 5 minutes more, until the crabs are cooked. Remove excess liquid before serving.

Helpful hint: Large shrimp can be substituted for the crabs if these are more readily available.

HOI MA-LAENG POO OB

Steamed Mussels

Beautiful orange-fleshed green-lipped mussels contrast with the bright green basil leaves in this simple but excellent seafood dish. ② ①

4½ pounds mussels, cleaned well
Large handful basil leaves (*horapa*)

Sauce:
½ cup lime juice
2 tablespoons fish sauce
1 teaspoon sugar
2 cilantro roots, chopped
2 cloves garlic, crushed
½ cup water

Place the mussels in a steamer over boiling water and sprinkle with the basil leaves. Steam for 10 minutes. Remove from the heat and wait for 2 minutes before opening the steamer.

Meanwhile, mix the sauce ingredients together, bring to a boil, then leave to cool.

Serve the mussels accompanied by the sauce, used for dipping.

Helpful hint: Leaving the mussels to sit covered for a couple of minutes after steaming helps the flavor of basil to permeate the mussels.

TAUD MAN GOONG
Deep-fried Shrimp Cakes

Hawkers in coastal towns, especially around Songkhla, Surat Thani and Phuket, offer a similar but highly seasoned snack made with fish (Taud Man Pla). This more delicate version prepared with shrimp is served with a savory accompaniment of pickled vegetables. ◑◑

1¼ pounds large shrimp
5 ounces lard
1 teaspoon salt
½ teaspoon sugar
2 cups fresh bread crumbs
4 cups oil

Accompaniment:

1 cup distilled white vinegar
½ cup sugar
5 bird's-eye chilies
2 shallots, sliced
1 tablespoon finely sliced cauliflower
1 tablespoon finely sliced baby corn
1 tablespoon sliced small cucumber

To prepare the **accompaniment**, bring the vinegar and sugar to a boil, then leave to cool. Add all vegetables, mix and set aside.

Chop shrimp and lard together or process in a blender until fine. Add salt, sugar and bread crumbs, then shape into patties. Deep fry in the oil until golden brown and fragrant.

Serve hot with the accompaniment.

Helpful hint: The accompaniment and shrimp cakes can be prepared in advance. Fry the shrimp cakes just before serving.

POO JAA

Deep-fried Stuffed Crab Shell

Use either mud crabs or blue swimmer crabs for this dish. The filling can be prepared in advance and the crabs stuffed and deep fried just before serving. ⏱ ⏱

4 whole crabs
3 eggs, well beaten
5 cups oil
1 tablespoon cilantro leaves
2 red chilies, cut into lengthwise strips

Stuffing:
6 ounces ground pork ($^{1}/_{2}$ cup)
$^{1}/_{3}$ cup minced shrimp (7 large)
$^{1}/_{2}$ cup fresh crabmeat
2 tablespoons chopped onion
1 tablespoon finely sliced spring onion
1 teaspoon ground white pepper
1 teaspoon sugar
$^{1}/_{4}$ teaspoon light soy sauce
$^{1}/_{4}$ teaspoon salt

If using cooked crabs, remove the backs carefully and discard any spongy matter. Wash backs and set aside. Remove crabmeat from body, legs and claws and measure out $^{1}/_{2}$ cup, keeping the rest aside for another dish.

If using raw crabs, steam first, then prepare as directed above.

Mix all the stuffing ingredients together and fill the crab shells.

Heat the oil in a pan, dip the stuffed crabs in the beaten egg to coat them well all over and then deep fry for about 10–15 minutes until cooked. Remove and drain well on paper towels. Sprinkle with cilantro and chilies before serving.

HOY LAI PED

Fried Clams in Roasted Chili Paste

Use any type of clams for this emphatic, quickly prepared dish. It's worth hunting for the right type of basil, as it makes a definite difference to the flavor of the clams. ☯ ☯

$^1/_3$ cup oil
$1^1/_4$ pounds clams in their shells, cleaned well
$1^1/_2$ tablespoons chopped garlic
5 fresh red chilies, sliced lengthwise
2 tablespoons roasted chili paste (page 38)
2 teaspoons light soy sauce
$^1/_2$ cup chicken stock (page 41)
Large handful basil leaves (*horapa*)

Heat the oil in wok, add the clams and garlic and cook until the clams open slightly. Add the fresh chilies, chili paste and soy sauce, mix well, then add chicken stock. Stir in the basil and serve immediately, accompanied by rice.

Helpful hint: Soak the clams in several changes of water for an hour or so before cooking to ensure they are thoroughly clean.

HAW MOK THALAY
Steamed Seafood Cakes

A universally popular dish well worth the time needed to prepare it, this mixture of seafood, coconut milk and seasonings is steamed in small cups made of banana leaf. It is possible to use small ramekins or any other small heatproof dishes as a substitute. ☺ ☺ ☺

$^3/_4$ cup coconut cream
1 teaspoon rice flour (available where Asian foods are sold)
4 ounces filleted fish, cut into thin slices
4 ounces shrimp, peeled and cleaned
4 ounces squid, cleaned and cut into 2-inch pieces
1 egg
3 tablespoons fish sauce
$1^1/_4$ cups coconut milk
$^1/_2$ cup basil leaves (*horapa*)
2 tablespoons shredded kaffir lime leaves
Fresh cilantro to garnish
1 finely sliced red chili
Banana leaf cups 2 inches square, or individual ramekins

Spice Paste:
5 dried chilies, soaked in water and deseeded
3 cloves garlic
2 tablespoons finely sliced galangal
1 teaspoon grated kaffir lime rind
2 teaspoons finely sliced cilantro root
5 black peppercorns
$^1/_2$ teaspoon salt
1 teaspoon shrimp paste
1 teaspoon finely sliced *krachai*, optional

Pound the **spice paste** ingredients well in a mortar or process in a blender.

Mix coconut cream with the rice flour and bring to a boil, stirring until thickened. Remove from the heat, cool and set aside for topping.

Mix the spice paste with the fish, prawn, squid, egg, fish sauce and then add the remaining coconut milk, a little at a time. Add half the basil and kaffir lime leaves and mix in.

Place one of the remaining basil leaves in the bottom of each cup, top with the fish mixture, cover and steam for 15 minutes. Remove the cups from steamer, and top each one with a little of the boiled coconut cream, cilantro leaf, kaffir lime leaf and sliced chili. Return to the steamer, cook for 1 more minute, then remove from the steamer.

PLA CHORN PHAD PRIK KHING

Crispy Fish with Red Curry Sauce

Pla chorn, a fish that is similar to Spanish mackerel, is preferred for this recipe where the fish pieces are fried until crisp and topped with a thick, spicy sauce. Any firm-textured white fish can be used as a substitute. ⏱

2 tablespoons red curry paste (page 38)
1 cup coconut milk
Fish sauce to taste
1 teaspoon sugar, or to taste
2 tablespoons dried prawns or shrimp, ground
$^3/_4$ pound fish fillets or steaks
Oil for deep frying
1–2 long beans, cut in $^3/_4$-inch lengths
   (optional)
1 kaffir lime leaf, finely shredded

Fry the curry paste in coconut milk until the sauce thickens, then add the fish sauce and sugar to taste. Add the dried prawns or shrimp.

Dry the fish thoroughly, then deep fry in very hot oil until crisp and golden. Set aside.

To serve, put the crispy fish on the plate. Top with the sauce and scatter with long beans (if using) and shredded lime leaf.

PLA NUEA ORN

River Fish with Chili Sauce

Although freshwater fish are preferred for this dish in Thailand, any good white-fleshed sea fish can be used instead. ⊘⊘

- **1 whole freshwater fish weighing about 2 pounds, or 2 smaller fish**
- **5 ounces dried red chilies, soaked in the water and deseeded**
- **$\frac{1}{2}$ cup garlic, peeled**
- **$\frac{1}{2}$ cup shallots, peeled**
- **1 tablespoon shrimp paste**
- **4 cups oil**
- **Fish sauce to taste**
- **1 teaspoon sugar**
- **10 kaffir lime leaves, very finely shredded**

Scale and clean the fish thoroughly, leaving on the head if liked. Make cuts about $\frac{1}{2}$ inch deep along the back of each fish to give them a decorative appearance.

Finely chop the chilies, garlic and shallot, then mix with the shrimp paste. Fry in 3 tablespoons of oil until fragrant, then add fish sauce and sugar.

Dry the fish thoroughly, then deep fry until cooked. Put on a serving plate topped with the sauce. Sprinkle with kaffir lime leaves and serve immediately.

PLA SAMLEE DAD DEOW

Deep-fried Fish with Mango Salad

The sour tang of unripe mangoes mixed with other seasonings enhances the flavor of fresh fried fish. Use any firm-textured white fish. ◑ ◑

1 small fresh fish, weighing about 10 ounces
2 cups oil
¹/₂ large green unripe mango, cut in matchsticks (1 cup)
3 tablespoons sliced shallots
5 red or green bird's-eye chilies, chopped
1 tablespoon chopped palm sugar, or to taste
Fish sauce to taste
Lime juice to taste
¹/₄ cup roasted cashew nuts, to garnish

Clean and scale the fish, removing the head. Cut lengthwise from underneath and carefully remove the backbone and all other bones. Dry thoroughly and set aside.

Mix all other ingredients together. Taste and add a little fish sauce if not sufficiently salty; if not sour enough, add lime juice.

Deep fry the fish in hot oil until crisp and golden. Drain and serve the fish with the mango garnish arranged in the center. Scatter with roasted cashew nuts.

KAI YAD SAI

Savory Stuffed Omelets

Frequently found on the menu of simple restaurants as well as at roadside stalls, this is often eaten at lunch time. The omelet can also be served with rice as part of a main meal. ✦ ✦

$\frac{1}{4}$ **cup oil**
4 ounces ground pork
3 tablespoons diced tomatoes
3 tablespoons cooked green peas
2 tablespoons finely diced onion
$\frac{1}{2}$ **tablespoon sugar**
1 tablespoon fish sauce
$\frac{1}{4}$ **teaspoon ground white pepper**
$\frac{1}{4}$ **teaspoon black soy sauce**
3 eggs, beaten
3 tablespoons chopped cilantro leaves
1 red chili, sliced

Heat half of the oil in a wok over high heat and stir fry the pork for 2 minutes. Add all the remaining ingredients except for the eggs, cilantro, chili and remaining oil. Fry until cooked then set aside.

Heat an omelet pan (6–8 inches) in diameter, add a drop of the remaining oil. Pour in enough egg to thinly cover the base. Brown the omelet lightly on both sides, flipping over halfway through cooking. Repeat until all the egg is used up.

To stuff the omelets, place a spoonful of pork mixture in the center, fold two opposite sides toward the center and then fold in the remaining sides so that it resembles a square. Put onto a serving plate and repeat until all the egg and pork mixture is used up.

Garnish with cilantro leaves and finely sliced red chili. Serve accompanied by rice.

GAENG KHEOW WAN GAI

Green Chicken Curry

A fragrant, creamy curry which is always popular. Remove the skin from the chicken if you wish to reduce the fat. 🕐 🕐

1/2 cup coconut cream
3 tablespoons green curry paste (page 38)
12 ounces chicken breast, sliced
2 cups coconut milk
2 kaffir lime leaves
1 1/2 tablespoons fish sauce
1 teaspoon sugar
1 1/3 cups eggplant, cut into bite-sized pieces
1/4 cup basil leaves (*horapa*)
2–3 red chilies, cut in lengthwise strips

Heat coconut cream until it begins to have an oily sheen, then add the curry paste and stir well. Add the chicken and cook until it changes color.

Add coconut milk, lime leaves, fish sauce and sugar. Bring to a boil, then add the eggplant. Simmer until the chicken is cooked, then add the basil and chilies. Remove from heat and serve.

Helpful hints: This dish can be prepared in advance by cooking it until the chicken is tender. Add the basil and chilies when reheating the dish just before serving.

GAI HOR BAI TOEY & GAI YANG
Chicken Fried in Pandan Leaves & Barbecued Chicken

CHICKEN FRIED IN PANDAN LEAVES

Fragrant screwpine or pandan leaves add their subtle fragrance to this fried chicken. ☺☺

2 pounds chicken thighs
20 pandan leaves
Oil for deep frying

Marinade:

Opposite:
*Gai Hor Bai Toey
(Gai Yang is not
photographed)*.

2 tablespoons light soy sauce
2 tablespoons oyster sauce
1 teaspoon sugar
2 teaspoons sesame oil
**1 teaspoon each garlic and cilantro root,
    pounded together to a paste**

Sauce:

1 cup distilled white vinegar
$\frac{1}{2}$ cup sugar
2 tablespoons black soy sauce
1 teaspoon white sesame seeds, fried
$\frac{1}{4}$ teaspoon salt

Debone chicken and cut thighs into 4 pieces. Mix **marinade** and marinate the chicken meat for 3 hours. Mix **sauce** ingredients together and set aside.

Wrap two or three pieces of chicken with pandan leaves to form a bundle (see photo). Deep fry until fragrant. Serve with dipping sauce and steamed rice. (Omit pandan leaves if not available.)

BARBECUED CHICKEN

A northeastern version of a dish found all over the country. ☺☺

1 chicken ($2\frac{1}{2}$ pounds), cut in large pieces

Marinade:

10 cloves garlic, finely chopped
2 tablespoons black peppercorns, crushed
2 tablespoons light soy sauce
2 tablespoons sugar
2 tablespoons brandy or dry sherry
1 teaspoon salt

Sauce:

1 cup distilled white vinegar
$\frac{1}{2}$ cup sugar
3 cloves garlic, coarsely chopped
2 red chilies, finely pounded
1 teaspoon salt

Mix chicken with the marinade and leave for 3–4 hours. Mix all sauce ingredients, bring to a boil and simmer until thick. Cool.

Grill chicken over hot charcoal or under a grill, turning from time to time, until cooked. Serve the chicken accompanied by plain or glutinous rice and Som Tam (page 72).

GAENG PED GAI NAW MAI

Red Chicken Curry with Bamboo Shoots

Fresh bamboo shoots are a seasonal vegetable in Thailand, and have a sweetness and texture that cannot quite be matched by the canned variety. However, the latter make an acceptable substitute, providing a firm contrast to the tender chicken in this curry-style dish. ➊ ➊

$\frac{1}{2}$ cup coconut cream
1 tablespoon red curry paste (page 38)
12 ounces boneless chicken, diced
$1\frac{1}{2}$ cups coconut milk
10 ounces bamboo shoots (sliced lengthwise) (2 cups)
2 tablespoons fish sauce
$\frac{1}{4}$ teaspoon salt
$1\frac{1}{2}$ teaspoons sugar
5 kaffir lime leaves, halved
1 fresh red chili, finely sliced lengthwise
$\frac{1}{2}$ cup basil leaves (*horapa*)

In a pot, bring the coconut cream to a boil. Simmer, stirring constantly, until the surface takes on an oily sheen. Put in the red curry paste and chicken, stir well, and add coconut milk and bamboo shoots.

Cook until the chicken is tender, then add fish sauce, salt, sugar, kaffir lime leaves and chili. Remove from heat and garnish with basil.

Helpful hints: If using canned bamboo shoots, drain and boil in fresh water for about 5 minutes to get rid of any metallic taste. Fresh bamboo shoots should be sliced and simmered until just tender before being added to the curry.

GAENG PED
Roast Duck Curry

Seasoned red-roasted duck sold by Chinese restaurants and food stores is the basis for this richly flavored curry. ◑◑

1 roasted duck
$\frac{1}{2}$ cup coconut cream
3 tablespoons red curry paste (page 38)
2 cups coconut milk
2–3 large tomatoes, in wedges
1 cup green beans cut in $\frac{1}{2}$-inch slices
4 kaffir lime leaves
2 tablespoons fish sauce
1 teaspoon sugar
$\frac{1}{2}$ teaspoon salt
10 basil leaves (*horapa*)
4 red or green chilies, cut into fine lengthwise strips

Remove all bones from the duck and cut the meat into bite-sized pieces.

Heat the coconut cream over medium heat and add the red curry paste, stirring well. Add the duck and stir well, then add the remaining coconut milk, tomatoes, green beans, kaffir lime leaves, fish sauce, sugar and salt. Bring to a boil, then remove from heat.

Sprinkle with the basil leaves and red or green chilies. Serve with plain rice.

Helpful hint: The green beans add a slightly crunchy texture to the smooth curry.

KHA KOB PHAD PED

Frogs' Legs with Chili and Basil

Frogs, found in the *klongs* or canals and rice paddies of Thailand, are sometimes euphemistically called "paddy chicken." Their flavor is delicate and similar to chicken. ◷◷

> ⅓ cup oil
> 8 pairs of frogs' legs
> 1 tablespoon green peppercorns
> 3 red chilies, sliced lengthwise
> 3 inches galangal, cut into fine matchsticks
> 2 teaspoons fish sauce
> ½ teaspoon chopped palm sugar
> Large handful basil leaves (*horapa*)

Heat the oil in a wok until very hot. Add frogs' legs and peppercorns and stir fry over high heat for a couple of minutes. Add chilies, galangal, fish sauce and sugar. Mix well and cook for another minute. Stir in the basil, take off the heat and serve.

Serve accompanied by rice.

Helpful hint: 8 ounces boneless diced chicken can be substituted for the frogs' legs.

KAW MOO YANG

Pork Neck with Chili Sauce

The common Thai seasoning of garlic, black pepper and cilantro root is partnered with Chinese oyster and soy sauces to marinate the pork, which is then grilled and served with a spicy sauce. ☺

1¼ pounds pork neck, in one piece

Marinade:

- **1 tablespoon each chopped garlic, cilantro root and black peppercorns, pounded together to a paste**
- **2 tablespoons oyster sauce**
- **2 tablespoons light soy sauce**
- **1 tablespoon sugar**

Sauce:

- **2 shallots, thinly sliced**
- **1 teaspoon chili powder**
- **1 tablespoon fish sauce**
- **1 tablespoon lime juice**

Mix all **marinade** ingredients together and marinate the pork for 1 hour.

While the pork is marinating, mix the **sauce** ingredients together and set aside.

Grill the pork over hot charcoal or under a very hot grill until the meat is cooked. Cut the pork in thin diagonal slices and put on a serving dish. Serve with sauce accompanied by steamed glutinous rice and sliced cucumber.

Helpful hint: If pork neck is not available, choose another cut of pork, such as loin, which has a thin layer of fat.

GAENG MUSSAMAN

Mussaman Beef Curry

Spices such as cardamom and cinnamon were brought to Thailand by Indian Muslim traders, and dishes using these are referred to as Mussaman (Muslim) curries. This version from southern Thailand uses the basic Mussaman curry paste and other spices. 🕐 🕐

3 tablespoons Mussaman curry paste (page 38)
$\frac{1}{2}$ cup coconut cream
1 pound beef sirloin or stewing beef
2 cups coconut milk
5 cardamom seeds, roasted until fragrant
1 cinnamon stick about 3 inches in length
2 medium-sized potatoes, peeled and cut into large chunks
1 heaped tablespoon unsalted peanuts, chopped
10 shallots
3 bay leaves
3 tablespoons chopped palm sugar
3 tablespoons fish sauce
3 tablespoons tamarind juice

Cook the curry paste and coconut cream together for 5 minutes, then add the beef and fry for 8–10 minutes. Add the rest of the coconut milk, bring to a boil and simmer gently for 10 minutes.

Add all the remaining ingredients and cook until the potatoes and meat are tender.

Serve accompanied by sliced pickled ginger, pickled vegetables and rice.

Helpful hint: The potatoes provide a contrast in texture and a bland counterpoint to the spicy gravy.

GAENG PED MOO

Red Pork Curry

Pork is the most popular meat in Thailand, prepared in many different ways. This is a very simple, quickly prepared curry. ◑◑

½ cup coconut cream
1 tablespoon red curry paste (page 38)
12 ounces pork tenderloin, cut in ½-inch slices
1½ cups coconut milk
2 tablespoons fish sauce
¼ teaspoon salt
1½ teaspoons sugar
5 kaffir lime leaves, halved
1 fresh red chili, finely sliced lengthwise
½ cup basil leaves (*horapa*)

Bring the coconut cream to a boil, stirring constantly. Put in the red curry paste and pork, stir well, and cook until done (about 5 minutes).

Add fish sauce, salt, sugar, kaffir lime leaves and chili. Stir and heat through, then remove from heat and garnish with basil.

Helpful hint: If pork fillet is not available, use any other lean cut of pork and increase the cooking time accordingly.

PANAENG NUEA
Dry Beef Curry

A southern style of cooking beef, hot and fragrant with typically Indian spices. The use of palm sugar, peanuts and kaffir lime leaves, however, is distinctly Thai. ⏲ ⏲

1 tablespoon coriander seeds, ground
2 teaspoons cumin seeds, ground
3 tablespoons Mussaman curry paste (page 38)
½ cup coconut cream
12 ounces beef, cut into thin strips
1½ cups coconut milk
½ cup ground roasted peanuts
2½ tablespoons fish sauce
¼ teaspoon salt
3 tablespoons chopped palm sugar
6 kaffir lime leaves, torn in half
1 red chili, thinly sliced

Mix the ground coriander and cumin with the Mussaman curry paste.

Heat coconut cream until some of the oil surfaces, then add the curry paste and slowly bring to a boil, stirring constantly.

Put in beef strips and cook for 5 minutes, add remaining coconut milk and the rest of ingredients, except for the kaffir lime leaves and chili. Stir well and simmer until the meat is tender.

Add the kaffir lime leaves and chili, remove from the heat and serve with white rice.

TAB TIM GROB & KLOEY BUAD CHEE
Red Rubies & Bananas in Coconut Milk

RED RUBIES

This rather poetic name is given to tiny diced water chestnuts colored bright red and served in sweetened coconut milk. One of the most popular Thai desserts. ⏱ ⏱

1 cup (about 8 ounces) finely diced water chestnuts
Red food coloring
$^1/_2$ cup tapioca starch (available where Asian foods are sold)
$^1/_2$ cup sugar
$^3/_4$ cup water
$^3/_4$ cup coconut milk
Crushed ice

Sprinkle the water chestnuts with red food coloring and stir until bright red. Put the tapioca starch in a plastic bag and add the water chestnuts and shake so the pieces become well coated. Put in a colander or sieve and shake to allow excess flour to fall away.

Bring 5 cups water to a boil, add the water chestnuts and simmer for 3 minutes. Drain and plunge in cold water. Drain again and set aside on a cloth.

Boil the sugar and the water to make syrup, allow to cool, then add the coconut milk. To serve, put a little of the water chestnut into dessert dishes and add some of the syrup and ice. Additional slices of ripe jackfruit or young coconut can be added if these are available.

Helpful hints: Although troublesome to peel, fresh water chestnuts have a delicate sweetness and excellent texture. If these are unavailable, jicama can be substituted.

BANANAS IN COCONUT MILK

There are more than a dozen different types of bananas in Thailand; this recipe uses the tiny sweet variety sometimes known as finger bananas or lady finger bananas abroad. If using large bananas, cut on the diagonal into 3-inch lengths. ⏱

4 cups thin coconut milk
1 cup sugar
$^1/_4$ teaspoon salt
3 small bananas, cut diagonally in half

Pour the coconut milk into a pot, add the sugar and salt. Bring to a boil, stirring constantly to prevent the coconut milk from separating. Add the bananas, return to a boil, and then remove from the heat. Serve hot or cold.

Opposite:
Tab Tim Grob (top), Kloey Buad Chee (right) and Bua Loi (left). Recipe for Bua Loi is on page 126.

SANGKAYA FAK THONG & BUA LOI

Pumpkin Custard & Rice Balls in Coconut Milk

Opposite:
*Sangkaya Fak
Thong.
Photograph of
Bua Loi is on
page 125.*

PUMPKIN CUSTARD

A decorative dessert where a rich coconut-milk custard is steamed inside small pumpkins. ⏱

5 eggs (2 of them duck eggs if possible)
1 cup coconut cream
1 cup chopped palm sugar or $^1/_2$–$^3/_4$ cup
   white sugar
1 whole small pumpkin, about 8 inches
   in diameter

Beat the eggs with coconut cream and sugar until the mixture is frothy.

Cut the top off the pumpkin and carefully scoop out the seeds and any fibers. Pour in the coconut cream mixture, cover with the top of the pumpkin and place in a steamer. Cover the steamer and place over boiling water. Cook for about 20 minutes or until the mixture has set.

Leave to cool and cut in thick slices to serve.

Helpful hints: The duck eggs add richness and a firmer texture to the custard. If using palm sugar, strain the custard through a sieve before pouring into the pumpkin.

RICE BALLS IN COCONUT MILK

A simple, inexpensive dish in Thailand where glutinous or sticky rice flour and coconut milk are readily available. ⏱⏱

3 cups glutinous rice flour (available where
   Asian foods are sold)
4 cups coconut cream
2 cups sugar
1 teaspoon salt

Mix the rice flour with enough water to make a stiff paste. Knead well and then form into pea-sized balls. Bring a large pot of water to a boil, toss in the balls and remove when they float to the surface. Drain.

Bring half the coconut cream to a boil, stirring constantly to prevent it from separating, then add the flour balls. When the mixture returns to a boil, remove from the heat and stir in the remaining coconut cream. Serve as dessert in small bowls.

Helpful hints: Canned sweet corn kernels and cooked, colored diced water chestnut (prepared as for Red Rubies, page 124) can be added to the Rice Balls in Coconut Milk if you want a more varied and colorful dessert.

KHAO MAO TOD & KAO TOM MAD

Deep-fried Bananas & Bananas in Glutinous Rice

Opposite:
*Kao Tom Mad
(left) and Khao
Mao Tod (right).*

DEEP-FRIED BANANAS

Bananas are rolled in a mixture of rice flakes, grated coconut and palm sugar before being dipped in batter and deep-fried. ☺ ☺

1$\frac{1}{4}$ pounds freshly grated coconut
1 cup palm sugar, chopped
12 ounces rice flakes (*khoa mao*)
10 small finger bananas

Batter:

3 cups glutinous rice flour (available in Asian
  food markets)
1 cup coconut milk
1 egg, lightly beaten
1 tablespoon sesame seeds

Combine the coconut, palm sugar and rice flakes and sauté in a nonstick pan, stirring frequently, for $\frac{1}{2}$ hour. Set aside. Mix the batter ingredients and let it stand for 3 hours.

Just before serving, roll each banana in the sautéed mixture, then dip in the batter and fry in the hot oil until golden brown. Serve hot.

Helpful hints: Flattened rice grains or rice flakes are found under a variety of names in most Asian countries, and are often known by the Filipino name, *pinipig*, abroad. Any type of rice flake or even wheat flake can be substituted.

BANANAS IN GLUTINOUS RICE

An interesting combination of glutinous rice, black beans and bananas. ☺ ☺

1$\frac{2}{3}$ cups glutinous or sweet rice, soaked in
  water for 1 hour
2 cups coconut cream
4 tablespoons sugar
Pinch of salt
8 ounces dried black beans, soaked overnight
  then boiled until soft
4 small fat bananas, halved
8 pieces banana leaf or aluminum foil, about
  6 inches x 10 inches

Mix the soaked, drained glutinous rice with coconut cream, sugar and salt and bring to the boil, preferably in a nonstick pan. Simmer, stirring frequently, until the rice is tender and all the coconut milk absorbed. This should take about 15 minutes. Leave to cool.

Take a piece of banana leaf and put in a little of the rice mixed with a heaped teaspoonful of black beans. Place a banana half on top, cover with more rice and black beans, then fold up the banana leaf and tie securely. Repeat until all bananas are used up. Steam for 15 minutes, cool and unwrap to serve.

Mail-order Sources of Ingredients

The ingredients used in this book can all be found in markets featuring the foods of Southeast Asia. Many of them can also be found in any well-stocked supermarket. Ingredients not found locally may be available from the mail-order markets listed below.

Anzen Importers
736 NE Union Ave.
Portland, OR 97232
Tel: 503-233-5111

Central Market
40th & Lamar St.
Austin, Texas
Tel: 512-206-1000

Dekalb World Farmers Market
3000 East Ponce De Leon
Decatur, GA 30034
Tel: 404-377-6401

Dean & Deluca
560 Broadway
New York, NY 10012
Tel: 800-221-7714 (outside NY);
800-431-1691 (in NY)

Gourmail, Inc.
816 Newton Road
Berwyn, PA 19312
Tel: 215-296-4620

House of Spices
76-17 Broadway
Jackson Heights
Queens, NY 11373
Tel: 718-507-4900

Kam Man Food Products
200 Canal Street
New York, NY 10013
Tel: 212-755-3566

Nancy's Specialty Market
P.O. Box 327
Wye Mills, MD 21679
Tel: 800-462-6291

Oriental Food Market and Cooking School
2801 Howard St.
Chicago, IL 60645
Tel: 312-274-2826

Oriental Market
502 Pampas Drive
Austin, TX 78752
Tel: 512-453-9058

Pacific Mercantile Company, Inc.
1925 Lawrence St.
Denver, CO 80202
Tel: 303-295-0293

Penn Herbs
603 North 2nd St.
Philadelphia, PA 19123
Tel: 800-523-9971

Rafal Spice Company
2521 Russell
Detroit, MI 48207
Tel: 313-259-6373

Siam Grocery
2745 Broadway
New York, NY 10025
Tel: 212-245-4660

Spice House
1048 N. Old World 3rd St.
Milwaukee, WI
Tel: 414-272-0977

Thailand Food Corp.
4821 N. Broadway St.
Chicago, IL 60640
Tel: 312-728-1199

Uwajimaya
PO Box 3003
Seattle, WA 98114
Tel: 206-624-6248

Vietnam Imports
922 W. Broad Street
Falls Church, VA 22046
Tel: 703-534-9441

Index